Voices of Conflict
TEENAGERS THEMSELVES

Voices
TEENAGER

of Conflict

S THEMSELVES

compiled by the Glenbard East <u>Echo</u>
advised by Howard Spanogle

Adama Books   New York

Copyright © 1987 Adama Books
All rights reserved

Library of Congress Cataloging-in-Publication Data

Voices of conflict : teenagers themselves / compiled by the Glenbard
 East Echo ; advised by Howard Spanogle.
        p.   cm.
     Summary: Teenagers present their views on a number of
 controversial topics such as race, gangs, homosexuality, and the
 handicapped.
        ISBN 0-915361-94-9 : $16.95
     1. Youth—United States—Attitudes. [1. Youth—Attitudes.]
 I. Spanogle, Howard.   II. Echo (Lombard, Ill.)
 HQ796.V635   1987
 305.2′35′0973—dc19   87-19865
                                                                  CIP
                                                                  AC

Printed in Israel

Adama Books, 306 West 38 Street, New York, New York 10018

To previous Echo staffs
who pioneered our effort
to encourage communication between generations,
and to visionary friends
who have encouraged young journalists
to discover the voices of America.

Editor: Greg Jao

Associate Editors: Gina Nolan and Dave Seng

Copyeditor: Diana Slyfield

Contributing Writers: Eric Kammerer and Erik Landahl

Staff Writers: Doug Addison, Chris Anderson, Tim Burke, Sara Corrough, Doug Elwell, Michelle Jao, Cathy Mau, Kim Peirce, and Kathy Seagraves

Computer Coordinator: Robert Hester

Researchers: Mark Cerepa, Kevin Ellerbruch, Dave Landahl, Paulette Polinski, Jeannie Ryba, and Laura Ulfers

Research Assistants: Don Gomez, Chris Gorman, JoAnn Vasbinder

Art Editors: Mark Peaslee and Pete Mandik

Artists: Students from art departments at Glenbard East High School, Lyons Township High School-North Campus, and St. Charles High School

Book Design and Chapter Opening Decorations: Irwin Rosenhouse

Acknowledgments

Completion of **Voices of Conflict** was possible because of the vision and the generosity of the Village of Lombard, which provided the project a Community Development Grant; Malcolm Bilimoria, who designated the project as the recipient of a General Electric STAR grant; and the Book Benefactors: Gamit Enterprises, Grove Dental Associates, Prospect Federal Savings Bank, Standard Federal Savings and Loan Association, and Friends of the Helen M. Plum Memorial Library.

Additional assistance came from considerate librarians, who loaned us part of their air-conditioned facilities; a cooperative administration; Sharon Keller, who provided invaluable computer assistance; Lynne Doles, who fielded telephone calls and letters from throughout the nation; Ellen Steiskal, who photocopied the never-ending pages of copy and forms; bookstore manager Gerri Long; bookkeeper Blanche Knight; helpful secretaries; and supportive colleagues.

Hundreds of publications advisers as well as numerous scholastic journalism associations and high school principals provided essential assistance in conducting the discussions and in gathering the national reactions. In addition, *The Echo* is grateful for the support of its printer, CompuComp Corporation; the Youth Communication offices; the Glenbard East art department; the north campus art department of Lyons Township High School in LaGrange, Illinois; and the journalism department of St. Charles High School.

The staff especially thanks the families throughout this country who contributed to the project by serving as generous hosts and by assisting in the research process.

National reactions were gathered during 1986-1987 by the National Teenage Research Project, which was conducted by the *Glenbard East Echo*, a high school student newspaper in Lombard, Illinois. The opinions represent the diverse ideas expressed by nearly 4,000 teenagers. Though all individuals signed their comments, some names have been withheld because of the sensitive nature of the information. Editing changes have been made only in punctuation and spelling.

The discussions come from tape-recorded interviews. These interviews, conducted by *Echo* researchers and editors, were conversations with teenagers and adults in more than 28 cities throughout the United States. Adults have been distinguished by giving their last names to avoid confusion. Opinions expressed do not necessarily represent the views of their organizations or positions. Editing changes have been made only to avoid repetition or misrepresentation of an idea.

Contents

Preface

Reach out to America. Listen to the voices of conflict, of sincerity, and of dreams. Link teens and adults in a coast-to-coast conference call.

The conversation is so lively that the only way to make the conference call visible as well as audible is to take a carefully planned journed across America as well as a determined course toward completion of a second book.

So we went. By air, by rail, by interstate, by taxi, by rapid transit. During every school break, we were always rushing from our Lombard headquarters in Chicagoland to another corner of America.

Always teenagers themselves were looking for the texture of America: the reality, not simply the appearance, and the emotion, not simply the concept. Always there was another destination, another question, and another perspective—another way to link teenagers and adults.

The hookup entailed visits to schools, churches, youth centers, media centers, corporate offices, restaurants, homes—any place where honest teenagers and concerned adults were willing to talk. It also meant exhaustion, frustration, and drudgery, all rather understandable when these duties are added to publishing a newspaper, doing homework, and dealing with crises.

But the travel was only part of the research—the part that appeals to adventurous youth. The process also included a weekly discussion group at Glenbard East High School. In addition, thousands of teenagers submitted written responses for the book. And just about everyone, from the apprentice reporters to the editor-in-chief to the adviser's wife, found out how difficult it is to transcribe the hundreds of tapes.

During the summer, sixteen teenagers tapped the national hookup. The labored daily in a library classroom/mini-computer center, thanks to the cooperation of administrators and librarians. The summer crew juggled reams of paper, cassette recorders, tapes, and batteries. As teenagers listened to the concerns of America, the voices on the tapes became friends and commentators on conflicts with peers.

So they wrote. The research became more than memory and sound; it became an expression of creative essays and of diverse artwork. It became a documentary of American teenagers, an opportunity to communicate the conflicts so that adults and teenagers may reach out for solutions.

In *Teenagers Themselves,* the first book, connection was one-way—from teenagers to the world. In *Voices of Conflict,* teenagers converse with adults as well as with peers.

So listen in. Share the sounds and dreams with your community. Hear the concerns of teenagers.

Howard Spanogle
Adviser, Glenbard East *Echo*

Chapter 1.

Appearance and Reality

The magic kit came in the mail the second week in August. Ralph's little brother ordered it off a box of his favorite cereal, Frosted Finks, little sugar-coated criminals made of caramel and chemicals. Ralph tried a bowl once. He didn't sleep for three days.

Since his little brother was out burning off sugar energy, probably by shooting squirrels or by setting fire to the railroad tracks, Ralph unwrapped the package. The contents looked like most of the stuff he had sent for as a kid—brightly colored, tightly wrapped, and much smaller than expected.

There were three items. The first, the "Box of Miracles," was an orange cardboard box with two holes in one side. Then there was the "Wonder Rope," indeed a rope but one that looked quite plain and unwonderful. The real zinger of the bunch, though, was the "Future Globe," a kind of glass baseball filled with bright colors that flashed and glowed. Ralph couldn't take his eyes off the globe, which shifted and swirled, snapped and sparkled. In it he could almost see crystal facets and shadowy shapes moving across fields of maroon.

Whoa, Ralph thought. Enough. He put the globe back in the box and grabbed *Sports Illustrated* from the table. The sofa beckoned. He barely made it past the contents page before he faded into a luxuriant nap.

Usually anything short of a head-on airplane collision failed to wake up Ralph. But this afternoon he awoke slowly, ponderously, as if his eyelids were climbing Everest. The slow process was lucky for Ralph, for he was nose to nose with an intruder. Ralph didn't yell. He merely watched as a tall man draped in a black cape glowered at him with beady eyes. His smile, under a droopy mustache, was garish and malicious. The man looked uncomfortably like Dudley Doright's old cartoon nemesis, Snidely Whiplash.

"Gr-r-reetings young man," the caped creature thundered, rising up to what seemed a great height.

"Uh, hi," Ralph replied, staring as he tried to make sure this was the same sofa where he had fallen asleep.

"Hi? Young fellow, you are in rare good fortune this afternoon. I, Throckmorton Dunderville, magician to the royal court of King Wazmo of Iceland, have come to share with you the secrets of life itself, as revealed by your recently arrived tools of the trade." Dunderville gestured grandly to the discarded package on the table.

"The directions are in the box," Ralph croaked, scratching his head and rubbing his eyes. As his vision cleared, Throckmorton Dunderville seemed less and less like a menacing nightmare and more and more like a dorky blowhard. Dunderville ignored him and went about lining up the props. He selected the Box of Miracles and held it out as if it were a holy relic.

"My friend, I have spent a lifetime engaged in the art of illusion. I am a master of deceptive appearances. Lately I have come to wonder what illusion hath wrought upon the young of our world."

"Huh?" Ralph said.

"Look in here," Dunderville barked, his smooth upper-crust delivery showing traces of the Bronx. Ralph snapped to attention and bent to look into the eyeholes on the Box of Miracles.

"What do you see?"

Ralph saw a bunch of missiles rising out of a wheat field. He told Dunderville so.

"What are they for?"

"Well, defense. They make us stronger and scare the other guys. That way they don't get us first, and there's peace." It sounded right to Ralph. He heard it on the evening news all the time.

"Ah, I see." Dunderville smiled. "Peace weapons. And what do you make of those wheat fields, my boy? Those farmers are starving once again."

"They're having those concerts," Ralph asserted. "If they raise a couple of million, the whole thing will blow over. Same with the famine stuff, and the floods, and the poor people. All they need is money, right?"

Dunderville twirled his mustache by way of reply. Then, without warning, he snatched up the Wonder Rope and twirled it around Ralph's head. He drew the boy's head forward so they were nose to nose again.

"Sonny, they've been stringing you along. He punctuated each syllable with a sharp tug. "And you've been following them like a lemming." Dunderville's face contorted with missionary zeal.

"My ears are getting rope burn," Ralph said.

"Pardon me, young sir. I get carried away. But you must realize the hoax that is being perpetrated. In America, you all think you can throw piles of money at any trouble and squash it like a bug. Look at the advertisements—fancy people, fancy cars, fancy houses, and fancy lives. Look at your government, a stumbling dinosaur. Look at your own future. Will it be no more than a pointless groping for assets and tax deductions?"

Ralph stared blankly.

Dunderville spoke in rapid desperation. "Please, there are things you don't know yet, questions you haven't asked. You must examine what you're told. Don't give your trust cheaply."

There was something oddly touching about the magician's plea, Ralph thought.

WENDY OLSZEWSKI
LTHS

Appearance and Reality 13

Something pretty pathetic too. But, what the hell, he caught the guy's drift. He picked up the Future Globe and handed it to Dunderville.

"What's this one do?" he asked.

"This," Throckmorton Dunderville intoned, "is what will make the whole process, the whole struggle, worthwhile."

Ralph peered into the glowing orb and was enveloped in the warm sensations emanating from the colors. The moving shapes within focused for brief flashes. When he thought about them later, the images in the Future Globe didn't make much sense—a house on a hill, two children, and strangely, as if out of a dream, a tickertape parade. No, the images didn't make much sense, but his jangled nerves and rushing exhilaration somehow did.

Eric Kammerer

From Suburban to Urban

"If I've told you once, I've told you a thousand times. The city is a dangerous place."

"But Dad, I could really use the money this job can give me. Besides, it's in a good part of the city."

"There are no good parts of the city. It's full of muggers, drunks, homosexuals, thieves, and beggars. You're bound to get hurt if you go down there. It's no place for a teenage girl to work."

She couldn't handle this conversation anymore. For the past week her parents had been filling her with horror stories about the city. Granted, she was a little hesitant about taking a job there. She was scared, but she could never let her parents know that. She had to have the job. She needed the money—at least her parents agreed with her on that fact.

After hearing their endless tirades about the city, she had wild thoughts of her first trip there and of the people she would encounter. The bus that was supposed to drop her off at work would probably break down on the way. Of course, the crisis would occur in the worst part of the city. The passengers would have to get off. They would be forced to walk the rest of the way to their destinations. During her walk, she would encounter a beggar. He would trail after her, then hang on her arm and plead for money or food.

When she turned the next corner, a man would jump out and try to steal her purse. He would have long, stringy hair and broad shoulders. Other commuters would not stop to help. They would hear nothing and see nothing. The attack would turn out just the way her parents said it would.

While she walked along a deserted alley, two lesbians would follow her and then try to hit on her. Even thinking about it caused an embarrassing red flush to spread across her face.

Fearing for her life the entire time, she would end up running the last block to her office.

The vivid images in her mind made her break out in a nervous sweat. God, she was becoming as paranoid as her parents. But it was easy to be afraid when her life depended on the outcome of the trip. She tried to relax, but the fear was now instilled in her.

"Honey, do you still plan to go to the city?"

"Yes, Mom. I need the job, and I'll just have to take the chance. If something unexpected happens, I hope someone will help me."

"That's naive. You know your father and I don't want you to go. If you get hurt, don't expect us to pay the hospital bills."

Finally, the arguments were over. She had won. She would get on the bus at 7:30 A.M.

The air-conditioned bus made the start of her trip tolerable. She even arrived in the city on time. So far her nightmare had not come true. The three-block walk to her office was next. Somehow that scared her the most.

The first block of her journey proved to be harmless. It was actually pleasant. She began to feel a part of the city. She heard the piercing siren of a police car approaching. The officer was probably going to arrest a thief. Maybe that was one less criminal she had to look out for.

As she crossed the next street, she noticed men who looked like bums sitting in a doorway. They were not bothering people the way her parents said they did. She looked up at the street sign to make sure she was headed in the right direction. She didn't notice the man walking straight toward her. They collided. The impact stunned her. Her life would end in seconds. She had encountered a murderer on the street in broad daylight.

"I'm sorry miss. I didn't see you. Here's your purse. You dropped it."

She stood up in shock. The man she had bumped into was no murderer.

"Th-thank you."

She suddenly realized how wrong her parents had been. The city was similar to many other places, and people had to experience it to understand it. Her parents had kept themselves sheltered.

She walked into her building and took the elevator to the fourth floor. She was assigned a desk and introduced to other employees. A co-worker explained the company's filing system to her, and they discussed life in the suburbs while they worked.

"I'll never live in the suburbs," her co-worker said. "It would be terrible. There are no buses, no subways. . . no way to get around. Plus, with all those big, rich houses, I'd be afraid that I couldn't keep up with my neighbors."

She was amazed by the way he viewed the suburbs. People live their own lives. There are ways to get around. This guy was crazy.

By the end of the first week, she confidently took the shortcut that ran through the smaller side streets to the bus terminal. She had abandoned her dark closet and stepped into the light of a new world.

Gina Nolan

National Reactions—Conflicts

The American Dream. Propaganda. The two are related. American children see America as the best place to live. They don't realize that America is one of the hardest countries to live in—comparable to the Soviet Union, if not worse.

I see America as a struggle. There is always a battle. Adults see America as something to overcome to survive.

Life in America is something to "hurry up and get over with." In fact, it's just a nightmare.

Jennifer Deniega, 14
Flemington, New Jersey

I see America as a country that is a legend in its own time, but since it knows what a hero it is, the country is going to lay back, drink beer, and get lazy watching TV while thinking of all the things it's done in the past. . . .

Tim Langley, 16
Duncanville, Texas

My view of the government is clouded, confused by its many faces. It says it wants peace, but its oversize military budget. . . . They cut the budgets that serve the community. Why? That's all I want to know.

Tim Sniffin, 16
Brookfield, Connecticut

I see America with a fresher viewpoint than many of the adults I know. I react differently to different subjects because I still have most of my life to live, and I don't want to act out the dreams of my elders. I want to act out my dreams while I still can. . . .

I resent all the pressures that are being put upon me. Sometimes I wish I could be a Mbuti pygmy in Africa. . . .

I also hate old people that are so closed minded that they heap old stereotypes on us—like. . ."They're all promiscuous." Right. . . . Nobody should try and overlook the fact that we're all different. We're all good, and we're all bad. We're all human.

Matthew Scannell, 16
Deerfield, Massachusetts

WENDY KWIATKOWSKI
LTHS

The way I see America is different from the way an adult sees America in that my perspective is in terms of my individual self while an adult would see it as the country as a whole or the American people as a whole. . . .

When the news of the Libyan invasion came out, the first thing that my friends and I thought was "Wow. We'd better not get drafted if there's a war." I thought of ways to dodge being drafted.

My parents, on the other hand, . . .told me and my brothers and sisters about money, a possible threat of war, and discussed its advantages and disadvantages to our country.

Whenever my parents discuss anything in terms of the country, I always find myself interjecting comments as to how it affects me.

Ginley Regencia, 18
Fanwood, New Jersey

I sit quietly watching TV.
Ted Koppel is staring back at me.

The newsman says that terrorism's here,
And it will be even worse this time next
     year.
And on to the weather, cold and sneezy,
In Chernobyl it's 7000 degrees and breezy.

I turn off the set, feeling bleak and alone,
Remembering the children's cries and
     moans
When will this sadness come to an end?
When will our sad world be on the
     mend?

I live to hear Ted Koppel say,
"I'm sorry. There's nothing bad to
     report today."

Cristin Flynn, 15
Brookfield, Connecticut

The way I see America is that it is a great place to live and grow up. But adults see it as just another place to live.

Randy Knapchuck, 18
St. Clair Shores, Michigan

Adults see America today and compare it to what it was in the past. Young adults see it today and compare it to what we think we would make it, or at least, what we would like it to be.

Jacqueline Mitchell, 17
Phoenix, Arizona

I believe there is a minimal difference in both the way I and adults see America. The adults I have talked to, namely my parents, tell me that America is full of people out to take what you have and won't stop at anything to get it. . . .

I would have to agree with my parents' theory because I have seen people try to do this, especially to my father who is a very aggressive businessman. . . .

I believe America is a land of opportunity, but you have to know how to apply it.

Henry Boucher, 15
Deerfield, Massachusetts

When I think of America, I think of red, white, and blue; stars and stripes; and our native history. We have the freedom of religion and freedom of speech and press. . . .

If this country were totally free, it would also be full of a lot more chaos than there is. . . . I personally would not want to be anywhere but here. I feel safe here, happy here, and free here.

Jeannette Cole, 19
St. Clair Shores, Michigan

The teens of America see their homeland crumbling around them. Rampant crime, unemployment, drug abuse, and moral decay cause the future for our generation to look bleak. We see men lying in the streets for want of a house but simply glance away.

We seem to grow more calloused each day, yet this seems to be the only way to survive in this world where it is every man for himself, and it isn't women and children first. . . .

Our generation has seen nothing but war and hatred among the people of the world. It seems that any madman with a gun or bomb can mold the consciousness of our nation. Men fight and die in wars that have little other reason to be fought than United States oil interests.

We live in the nuclear age, where power corrupts, bombs explode to cripple and maim children, and where petty tyrants can win millions of dollars in military aid.

We have seen the brave, new world, and it is as scary as hell.

> Ross Allen, 15
> Brookfield, Connecticut

America as I see it is whatever you want it to be. I see the country as a place where you can be free and live. . . .

> Trini Jackson, 16
> Dallas, Texas

I see America as a wonderful place to live. I would even die for it. My parents like it but are not willing to die for it.

> Todd Kunze, 15
> St. Clair Shores, Michigan

I see America as the best country in the world, a land of many freedoms. . . . No man is inferior to any other in America. I am proud of my country and would die for her to preserve the American way of life. . . .

I would rather live in America than anywhere else. It's the best country in the world—don't let anyone tell you otherwise. I'm damn proud of America: land of the free and the home of the brave. God bless it.

> Scott Tompkins, 14
> Brookfield Center, Connecticut

As a teenager, I see America through sad eyes. America is going downhill. It has got a number of problems with drugs and alcohol. The biggest problem I see is abortion and pornography. These two things are destroying America. Adults are talking about what war will do. . . . I don't think America will be destroyed by war. I think America is destroying itself with pornography.

> Ricky Hamb, 15
> Dallas, Texas

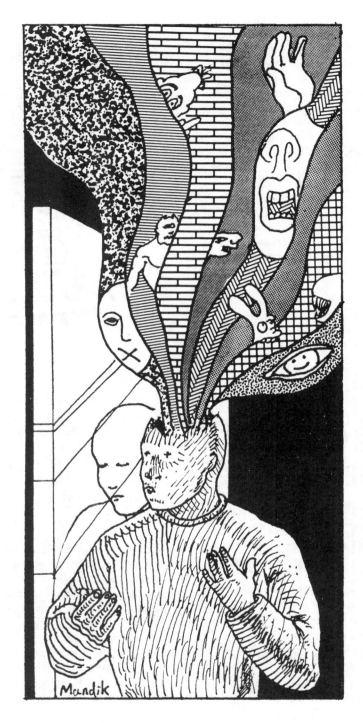

Reality can bring you down in the dumps. . . . Now the only way teenagers get away is by drinking beer or doing some kind of a drug. Most of the people here at Sandia High get drunk.

> Alan Longbotham, 16
> Albuquerque, New Mexico

The image of America is taking a degrading turn. America's hero is Rambo, a steroid-stud who takes the law into his own hands. Give him a machine gun, and his problems are solved. Ironically, our views on terrorism are quite similar.

> Michelle Stoll, 16
> North Little Rock, Arkansas

Discussion

Chicago
The New Expression office

What is the image of America?

Karriema: America is perfect. Americans are ideal. A "Brady Bunch" family. Land of the free, home of the brave.

Roberta: There are no problems. Americans always have money. They all have a place to live.

Lesley: Everyone loves everyone, no matter what color, race, or creed. If you come to America, all your problems will be solved.

Robin: It stands for justice, freedom, and the American way. And everyone has a piece of the pie, which is very untrue. People are going hungry and living on the streets.

Nicole: They are carrying all their possessions in paper bags. Some people have all the pie. Other people don't have any; they have the crust. America is synonymous with liberty and justice. But that's not true. The media make Americans ignorant because that's what they feed them. "America is this and that." America is always going to be ignorant because there are not enough people to tell them the truth. The people who know it are scared because there are not enough people who know it, and they will be labeled radicals.

Roberta: America mistreats its orphans, widows, and handicapped. America exploits everyone. Nothing about the image of America is true. It's either half-truths or a reasonable facsimile.

Robin: The reality is the black people are not free. We still have problems. We cannot live where we want to live even though we can afford it. We are still discriminated against. The Statue of Liberty is hogwash.

Karriema: It's just another statue. How can America be the land of freedom when at first the only way they got money was from slavery? But it's not just the blacks. Indians, Native Americans, are treated disgustingly. The government is moving Navajos off land that they have known all their lives because there is coal and oil down there.

Lesley: On "Donahue" this lady said, "If they can do it to us, don't you think they could do it to you?"

Roberta: It's not necessarily race; it's the underdog. The people who control the government and the money discriminate against everybody else.

Robin: There's a difference. If you are white and you have money, you can live anywhere and do anything. If you are black and have money, you can't live in Marquette Park [known for anti-black sentiment]. There are a lot of things that you can't do because of race. If you are white and have money, you can do anything you want to do.

Lesley: The rich get richer, and the poor get poorer.

Roberta: There are so many people. There are 100 opportunities for 1,000 people. Everybody doesn't get the same chance because if you are a certain social status, you may get the chance over someone who has the same skill. You have an opportunity, but it's not equal.

Tanya: It's not that they can never do it. It's just that it is harder.

Karriema: If somebody told me America was the land of opportunity, I would tell them, "You're very naive."

Roberta: We have more opportunity than anywhere else. That's why we are called the land of opportunity. Why do all these other people come over here? But even if people don't have equality, people should have enough food to eat. I would rather go out feeding everybody than worry about everybody's equal opportunity.

I don't believe in socialism because I don't want everybody to be equal. America gives you the opportunity to be over someone else.

Robin: I want to obtain the American dream.

Duncanville, Texas
The home of missionaries who worked in Colombia

Kerry: The biggest difference living here is the TV. We didn't have all that much television. Every Friday night we used to play cards. Now that we have gotten up here, we watch TV all the time. It's quick entertainment.

Anything you don't have a part in is not meaningful. When you watch TV, you say you're bored because you are not doing anything. You are just sitting there watching somebody else do something.

How did people react when they found out you were from Colombia?

Kerry: The first thing they ask is, "What did you do?" or, "Can you speak English?" A lot of times I am asked if I like America better. They don't understand when I say I really miss Colombia. A lot of kids say, "Don't you just love America? Isn't it the best?" It is in some ways, like we have a great government and everything. But it's not in a lot of ways.

Lorrie: I think America is lacking a little bit. Here the only thing people know how to do is write checks. Where we grew up in Colombia, our mother taught us more, such as how to sew and how to cook.

I don't think the world is becoming more materialistic. I think people are becoming lazier. I laughed so hard when I came up here. You can buy sweet rolls in a can. That kills me. I still can't get over that. You can buy grated cheese. You buy bread already mushed up for turkey. Things like that. It just kills me. It's not materialistic. They're just looking for an easy way out. Maybe it's better. They're saving time.

Sean: Americans want everything instant. They want it now—from microwave ovens to everything. They want instant fun. They want to go to school and get a degree. They want it now, but they don't want to put in the four years to get it.

What influences Americans?

Kerry: In American society, money is one of the main influences. It's not grades, it's just success. It's not how you get there, but just get there as fast as you can.

Lorrie: I know some kids who took some architecture classes in school. For their summer jobs, they were making $600 a week because they knew about architecture. Neither one of them wanted to go to school so that they could make more money. One guy goes from job to job. He doesn't want to go to school to learn more. He wants the money fast so he travels all over the country finding jobs where he can get a lot of money right away. When that job falls through, he'll go find another job.

San Francisco
Pacific News Service

Sandy Close (executive editor): There is no single America anymore. Twenty years ago you might have been able to say, "It's a dream of owning my own home, raising my family, and believing my children are going to do better than I did." That's what de Tocqueville said was unusual about America, that there was no great rich, no great poor, but this tremendous middle that had a sense of optimism.

The standard vision was of one life-style—the white suburban house with the picket fence, two cars, and a college education out there for the kids. Think of the enormous diversity of life-styles there is now. You can be gay in Castro. You can still be a hippie, flower child, or punk. You can live in Sun City with old people.

Watching the Martin Luther King memorial media coverage, you would think that it is a country of black and white, the way it was 20 years ago. In fact, the biggest minority in California is Latino followed by Filipino.

Latinos will become the largest minority in the country very soon. But it's almost as if there is a blank spot. The *San Francisco Chronicle* ran a story stating that San Francisco would become a Gaysian city, predominately of gays and Asians. It was done by a professor. Neither the editor nor the professor understood that the majority of minority kids in the San Francisco

public schools are Latino.

Americans are scared to death that once Latinos become American, Latinos will change the definition of what it means to be American. Latinos maybe think of themselves as Mexican American, Bolivian, Peruvian, or Trinidadian. If you ask, "What's common to all of you?" they will say, "We're American." The Latinos are not sure of who they are other than American.

The Associated Press editors put together a list of the ten most important foreign news stories of 1985, but Central America wasn't among them. There is a tendency not to understand that there is a historic movement of people going on from countryside to city, from country to country, from religion to religion, from field to factory. People are changing the way they live, the way they think, the way they've been living for hundreds of years, which is revolutionary. We've got this whole continent-and-a-half on the move. That's right in our midst, and yet we would not even include it in the ten most important stories. It's amazing.

What is unique about America?

Close: There has been a sense of moral purpose. Martin Luther King's greatness in many ways was that in the sixties he evoked that moral conscience in a way that no one else had done since Abe Lincoln and FDR. Now Tutu is touching it too.

We have a sense of optimism, of a God-given right to prosperity and to work. Now think about what the image of a permanent population of homeless people has done to the commonly shared vision of America. To survive as a parent with children, you either have to be very rich or very poor. But for a middle-class person, it's impossible. The cities are becoming more like third world cities. The Norman Rockwell America was small towns. They're disappearing. Suburbs are becoming either bedroom communities, or they're becoming sort of the refuge for the poor who have been pushed out of the cities. Or they're becoming increasingly wealthy.

Americans sensed that we'd eventually be able to absorb the pockets of poverty and become a great society. In 1964 the poverty program legislation was very revolutionary. It said government will provide a program that will eliminate poverty in America. Do you think anybody believes that now? No. In fact, we accept a condition of 7 percent unemployment as normal.

It's a tremendous change. It's very difficult for a lot of kids to know what they really will be. "If I don't get into MIT, UC-Berkeley, Loyola, or places like that, what's really ahead for me? Owning my own home? Probably not. Then how do I raise a family?" There is much more uncertainty.

How can people combat fear of change?
Close: There's no substitute for getting people to know individuals from these many different Americas. Two weeks ago, we put together a seminar of 20 Latino teenagers who dropped out of school and of three undocumented Latinos who came here at the age of 14. It was a way of putting a human face on their world. It made you feel that first of all, as humans, they weren't that different from you. You could relate to them. It drew you in without scaring you.

How should people redefine America?
Close: We are obviously on a threshold of a tremendous new ballpark. I don't think we're going to

DAN O'BRIE
LTH.

be able to revise the old nationalism to make everyone feel, "Rah rah America."

Somehow everybody says they're American, but they live in totally different ways. The big question is what will be the commonly shared idea. You can't say it's language. The majority of people in the city schools do not speak English at home.

Is it a sense that we all have a moral purpose or that we're all going to inherit the dream of the

American middle class? Nobody even thinks it's chic to be middle-class.

The best analogy in many ways is with Rome. Saint Paul was a Roman citizen. He had a Roman passport. He didn't speak Latin, but he could go all over the Roman Empire and take advantage of being a Roman citizen. But what did it mean beyond having that passport and feeling a part of that global system?

Maybe that is the direction we are headed. Being an American citizen is going to be a little bit like what it was for Paul being a Roman citizen.

Spring Hill, Tennessee
The Jenkins home

Peter Jenkins (author of *Walk Across America, Walk West, The Road Unseen* and *Across China*): Americans are people who don't really care about other cultures because we are so consumed by our own. A lot of countries don't like us because they think that we think we're too important to learn any other languages or understand any other ways of life. We live in such a big country, and we are not really confronted by other cultures.

What I've found in walking across America is that I had all those stereotypes like all southerners are rednecks and all Californians are fruits and on drugs. People from the Midwest drink 3.2 beers a day and go to football games. All Texans ride on horses and lasso Indians and stuff like that. A lot of that is based on the fact that a lot of Americans really don't know of these places.

These preconceptions are created by the media. Americans really believe that the media know what they are talking about. A lot of them, like Dan Rather and the people who write for the *New York Times*, sound very authoritarian and act like they know it all. But a lot of

them have tremendous biases and prejudices and lack of knowledge, yet they act as information transmitters for a lot of what we think.

One of the unfortunate things about a lot of Americans is that they take the interstates when they travel. It's not really like they're experiencing other cultures, other

parts of our society, or different kinds of people. Someone from Ohio or Illinois feels like they're going on a tremendous journey when they go to Disney World.

In all my speaking at colleges and universities, I notice that a lot of students want to travel, but most of them want to go to Europe. They think there is nothing to see in America. "It's just a bunch of shopping malls and McDonald's and subdivisions."

It's real important to have a sense of your own country, but our country is so big that it's not enough to know about suburban Chicago. I try to encourage people to take a year or a summer off and go to Colorado, go live in New York City, or go to Alabama.

It is unfortunate that a lot of people think they have to go straight through high school, college, and graduate school and start climbing the corporate ladder. They think that's the answer to it all. I think that it's important to know a little about yourself and where you fit into society. I think the only way that you can do that is by traveling and trying different things.

What does it mean to be an American?
Jenkins: It means that you are free. And freedom is a word that you don't appreciate until you have it taken away from you. It means just incredible opportunity to accept the challenge of life and do essentially whatever you can think of doing. It means an exciting future. I look at the world as an exciting place to

live, a place where you can try to change the things you don't like.

Duncanville, Texas

How important is the family?

Carol Keels (mother): Nothing competes with the family like American culture. You really have to fight for family time. We have to just say no. When you're living in a small community like we were living in, you can do everything available. You can plan a party, do everything possible, and still be bored. Having a relationship with anybody takes time. And the family is no exception. If you are really going to have a foundation, you are going to have to spend a lot of time together.

Kerry: In Colombia, everybody went home at 5 P.M., and everything shut down. But now, I'll come home from my piano lesson at 5, and Lorrie will be on her way to work. She'll come home after I go to bed. Then I'll go to school before she does so I hardly ever see her anymore. But in Colombia, I used to come home at 5 P.M., and everybody played basketball or something. Here, people work until all hours of the night.

What other problems are apparent?

Kerry: The hardest adjustment for me is how kids talk about everything. Their disrespect for elders, teachers, and parents. The terrible language, four-letter words. We never had that in Colombia at all. And the disrespect, just the way they talk about their parents. Kids hate them. That I don't understand.

Here, kids are getting married when they are still in high school, and they may be divorced by the time they are out of high school. They don't have to stay with that person. They don't think that they do. We learned how to stay with a person. How to change ourselves,

or how to help change something so that life can be more bearable.

Lorrie: Here, if I get mad at somebody, then there are a thousand more kids I can do something with. I don't have to do things with those kids. Down there, too bad. You're stuck. I could treat somebody badly, but I had to live with them for the next four years.

Kerry: I've had a problem making good, good friends. People are scared to make a commitment. You may talk to somebody in the hall. We have such quickie relationships. You don't really get to know people too well because you don't spend enough time with a person.

I'm used to spending more time to get to know people better. It's not a real relationship, as far as I'm concerned, when you see a person once a day for 50 minutes. When I get out of high school, I probably will never see half the kids that I've gotten to know. I may see them on the street and may say they look familiar. My friends from Colombia that I've spent so much time with— I'll keep in touch with them forever.

Washington, D.C.
Children's Defense Fund headquarters

What is the image of the American family?

Amy Tyler-Wilkins (staff member in the child care and family support services division): The average American family isn't what people think the average American family is. It's not "Father Knows Best" families anymore. It's not even two-parent families. It's not families where Mom stays home to take care of the kids. Your average family is a single-parent family.

Carol Holland (staff member in the education division): The administration would like the people to think it's apple pie and everything's wonderful. But there is a high percentage of single parents,

usually female-headed households. Kids drop out of school because they don't feel like being there anymore—"It's more exciting on the streets." Drugs are very exciting and a risk to take. Kids have a Mr. T mentality.

Tyler-Wilkins: Fifty percent of moms with kids under six are in the work force. That's what the reality is, rather than what the administration or sometimes the media would like us to think.

Holland: I think we underestimate the media. The media are very powerful. They will make you think what they want you to think. The newspapers really have to say only what people can stand to hear because they don't want hysteria to break loose in this country. Nobody really wants to hear the truth. It scares them.

Since the Vietnam War ended, people want to hear only good stuff. So the media minimizes the bad. Eventually, things get so bad that it's like a pimple. It starts getting bigger and bigger, and then suddenly it spurts out. The bad stuff was always there. All of the media try to throw you off to what's really going on.

Tyler-Wilkins: People are happier being comfortable deluding themselves, than they are being uncomfortable facing the truth. And even if the truth is this close to your nose, people will close their eyes and deny it. Everybody does that. But you'll deny it often to afford yourself an extra degree of comfort. And Ronald Reagan says, "America, we're standing tall, doing great, feeling good." They sugarcoat it, and we accept it.

It's this image of America that really never was. It's uncomfortable to deal with an unpleasant reality. They sugarcoat it, and we accept it. I'm not beyond wanting to delude myself. Then I have to look at statistics and say, "Jesus Christ, this is real."

Daniel Moynihan had this great line: "People believe that if you close your eyes to an issue, it'll go away." One issue that's true about is hungry kids. If you do close your eyes, they will go away. They'll die. You close your eyes, but the problem doesn't go away.

How can you encourage change?
Holland: A multifaceted approach must include lobbying to get legislation that starts to cut away at the facades that the administration is trying to give the American public. For us, it's working on policy, analyzing policy, doing editorials, and putting out publications to educate people. If you don't want to know the truth, you don't listen. So you are going to have those people out there who aren't going to listen to anything we say or anything we write about.

One approach is probably just pushing away and pounding away. You see the apartheid situation? The picketing and protesting outside the embassy is constant, nonstop. Unless you constantly put it in somebody's mind, it's never going to sink in. It's about the only way that you'll get something done. Or at least get people to think, "Oh, wow, there is something going on here." Even if they don't agree with our perspective, at least it is making them think.

Tyler-Wilkins: People don't want to believe that there are hungry children and poor children, that there are children who don't have homes, that there are children who are inadequately educated, and that there are parents who can't afford child care. But what you do is write it down, put it in books, and put it in the right people's hands.

Berkeley, California
University of California
Laura Nader (anthropology professor and member of the Carnegie Council): Americans don't put much into their children financially or otherwise in comparison to other industrialized nations. We put less into health, education, and welfare than any industrialized country.

Look at specifics like infant mortality: We have the highest rate among industrialized countries. We have ranked along with Portugal, Italy, Greece, with countries like Haiti. Our suicide rate among young people is high in this country. It's a symptom of the society. If you don't invest in children, that means you're really not investing in the future of the country. So I think it's a symptom of a larger malaise.

The high-tech industrialization that we have satisfies us materially, but it doesn't satisfy us emotionally. I think in many ways we are a depressed country—psychologically depressed—because we have all the things we ever aspired to have, but somehow there is something missing. I worry not just about kids committing suicide, but about the whole ethos, the whole society committing suicide. The dissatisfaction, the empty feeling that comes from solely emphasizing material progress or technological progress rather than social progress is related to denying the future. If we deny the future, we are clearly going to deny our children.

In the 1970s, the mandate of the Carnegie Council was to look at the state of American children. One question we asked was why people are always talking about parents vis-à-vis children instead of talking about the whole society as it's parenting children. We are all so interdependent now. When you say this to people, some people get upset because the psychologists have developed a model that says however the kid turns out is somehow the result of the parent. But the parents are living in a context which affects their ability to

be good parents.

We don't have a national family policy, a philosophy about how to deal with the family, as most industrialized countries do. People are trying to develop policy. Families are "in" again. Children are staying home longer for economic reasons as well as other reasons. And they are beginning to think that their best support structure is at home. The government is not going to support them. The corporate world is not going to support them. So maybe we ought to strengthen our roots, where we come from, whether they be neighborhood or family or both.

Spring Hill, Tennessee
How do stereotypes influence people?
Jenkins: Stereotypes, if you let them influence how you live, can be really injurious to your whole lifestyle. I grew up as a real preppy, and I used to have a real superiority attitude. If people didn't live in suburbia, belong to a country club, go to an Ivy League school, dress a certain way, talk a certain way, and look a certain way, somehow they just weren't adequate. I wouldn't associate with anybody who wasn't like me.

When I was a teenager, there was a period when everybody was putting down America. If I had believed in the stereotype and the image that the media and everyone were promoting, I would never have taken my walk, and I would never have found something different.

Why do people believe in stereotypes?

Jenkins: They're lazy. It's easier to say, "They're a bunch of rednecks, and they're a bunch of preppies. They're a bunch of blacks, and they're a bunch of Puerto Ricans. They're a bunch of hicks, and they're a bunch of snobs." It makes life less complicated. Plus, it's a challenge to make the time to get to know other people and find out where other people are coming from and what they're like. Lots of people like a nice, comfortable, orderly life where everything is cut-and-dry.

What are the most common misconceptions about teenagers?

Jenkins: "Every teenager is on drugs. Teenagers today don't care about this country. The Communists will just move in and take over because all that teenagers do is watch MTV and listen to Motley Crue." As in most stereotypes, there is an element of truth. Young people today are more diverse. When I was in high school, everybody looked a lot more similar. Today you can see people who look really punk. On the other hand, you can see people who are wearing sports coats to school. Then you have everybody in between. In the same school you have a Christian organization that's trying to save the campus. Also, you have this gay club and people playing rugby.

That's the way a free society should operate. Freedom of expression. If you can't express your feelings and opinions, then you can't really communicate. If you

can't communicate, then you're probably in trouble.

Boston
English High School

What causes stereotyping?

Huston Crayton (social studies teacher): The student picks up a biased opinion at home and brings it back to the school. For instance, getting food to Ethiopia because of the drought—most students didn't even know what caused the famine. They picked up from home that these people should stop having babies. "If Ethiopians would not have so many babies, then there would be enough food." One student mentioned the idea was from his mother.

"These people." "You people." These terms foster biases and racist ideas. "You people ought to clean your streets." We are all one people. We are all part of the human race. If we start separating ourselves ethnically and culturally, we have problems. Whenever someone comes up with "You people," it tells me that we're not together in the community.

I think that we need to start from scratch, teaching kids what an objective opinion is. How to debate. How to discuss. Use very light issues. Don't feed them steak and potatoes yet. Give them pabulum and milk, and let them get used to that. Then graduate them.

I don't think it's very hard to sit around and talk about racism in Roxbury or South Boston. I think it's hard to talk about the famine in Ethiopia when you don't even know where Ethiopia is. What is a famine? What are the politics of the region? These topics are hard even for grown-ups to discuss. How do you expect kids to do it? I think that they need to be fed something very basic. Something that affects them immediately. Then give them something that is more complex.

How deeply do teenagers care about issues?

Crayton: They really couldn't give a crap. They have this fatalistic attitude. It bothers me that they are so aware of nuclear proliferation, but they never talk about it. The kids are like, "Tomorrow may never come so let's live it up."

It would really make you sick to hear some of the things that they say. "Oh, all black people, all white people. . ." Very plain, raw statements are what they are living on. It's really pathetic. They really have the attitude that tomorrow will never come.

What else causes the apathy?

Crayton: I think there is a big breakdown in moral issues. We're living in a pluralistic society in which everything and anything goes. And the kids are taking this attitude. It's not being a fag; it's just alternative sex. There's no more adultery; it's just extramarital sex. There's no more genocide; it's displacement. Everything has a nice word.

Los Angeles
World Christian Training Center in Watts

What causes stereotyping?

Bill Seitz (national executive director): Not being aware of what's going on. People just adopt a view their parents have or their friends have of a particular situation.

A stereotype is very damaging when people of power, who do the hiring and who can help people who are disadvantaged, won't give people in the inner city a job because they stereotype.

If inner-city kids want to go into a certain area and all the doors slam because of their age or nationality, then they have to go to the school of hard knocks. You have to have role models around you to rise up and to succeed. Inner-city kids just figure,

"Hey, I just can't make it." They get a defeatist attitude early in life. When they can't go the positive route, they go the negative route.

Stereotypes get harder to break as you get older. For example, most of the groups we have visiting us here in the city are high school and college-age because they are not only more adventurous but also they're willing to fight through a lot of the stereotyping. The older people in the churches wouldn't do anything like that because they're set in their minds and in their ways.

Where do inner-city kids get images of suburbia?

Seitz: Television is their only frame of reference. Families they see on TV, like on "Family Ties," are their perceptions of a suburban family.

Los Angeles is a little different. You have inner-city kids who go to suburban schools. They don't have many misconceptions once they go to these schools and start meeting the young people. But as long as they stay in their own area, they tend to keep stereotypes.

How do inner-city kids differ from suburban kids?

Seitz: The average inner-city kid is more street-wise and independent than the average suburban kid because inner-city kids have to survive at an earlier age. A lot of times they don't have family backing. If they have parents, there may be a lot more kids in the family so the parents can't give the time to them. So they grow up quicker than people who live in the suburbs.

Is there a way to overcome stereotypes?

Seitz: You have to start with awareness. Once groups are aware of each other, then the continual helping out, the continual working together can start. Everybody can help each other.

I've found that to be my own case. The people here in Watts have given me so much more than I would ever be able to bestow upon them as far as knowledge or ways of doing things. That's the attitude you have to start with. It has to be a cross-cultural experience—not a snub from the inner city or a snub from the suburbs.

Compiled by Greg Jao

AMERICA—"DEFENDER OF HUMAN RIGHTS"

Solutions

I read...and I sometimes find myself putting me into the book. I don't know if it's to escape from reality, or if it is just to make the book more fun.... TV and movies provide a release valve to escape from the pressure and strain of the real world.

In a worse sense, drugs can take a person completely out of reality. The trips...supposedly help them. What they don't realize is that drugs are making reality worse, not better....

People need to escape. Without an escape, the real world becomes a burden. A person would spend too much time worrying and not have any fun in life.

Scott Hendrickson, 16
Grinnell, Iowa

One way that I try to escape reality is by writing. When I write, I can make the world happier. I can pretend there are no problems. I can create solutions to my problems. I enjoy making my own dream world.

Michelle Hertig, 17
Amity, Pennsylvania

My generation and generations to come are having a much harder time dealing with life. Not that we can't do it, but...

We have the fear of not having social security, of having to deal with major problems that our elders are creating for us, such as war and deterioration of our lands....

Most teens are forced to grow up too soon, and many aren't ready to grow up....

I don't want to die because this generation running the world now can't handle their job. How are we going to learn from them?...From their mistakes? What a terrible way to learn.

People need to escape from reality, to let off some pressure. If not, we'll deteriorate before it's our turn to pave the road for our children.

I bet if the adults running the world would seriously listen to teens,...life would be easier.

Carolyn Parady, 18
Clearwater, Florida

I've been into the party scene and thrown many bashes when the folks went out of town...in the quest for popularity. I think the real reason most people are attracted to this group is their apparent happiness.

"Everyone looks so happy." I've heard it and said it myself a million times. They seem to overlook that these people have problems too. The real reason people party is to try and escape their problems.... But the problem is there when they come off their "high."

I think the thing everyone is missing is God's love. With His love, such a great feeling is instilled that partying can be avoided. If more people would trust in the Lord, teen drug abuse and suicide could be avoided.

17-year-old male
New Mexico

I tried to escape my family and friends along with my emotions and problems by doing drugs for 2½ years. I was having lots of problems at school and home and wanted to get away from it all.

It took me 2½ years to realize that drugs weren't helping and were just making my problems worse. I pulled myself out of the drug situation and started working on my problems the right way.

15-year-old female
Florida

Chapter 2.

Whites and Blacks

In the 200 years since our Founding Fathers wrote the Declaration of Independence and the Constitution of the United States, our country has lost Something. Maybe I am a naive fool to believe that our Founding Fathers were serious about the Something that was supposed to make our country great. Maybe the Declaration and the Constitution are the first concrete examples of American propaganda.

Our country has lost the ideal of equality. It must have been hexed with the curse of "They" by some Puritan witch. They are not as good as We. They might have problems, but We don't care because They and We are mutually exclusive. The word They gives Us security. Where do They come from? Maybe They come from within. They are not Us.

"We Are the World," with its noble intentions, could smother the "They" curse that ravages this country. It is a wonderful ideal to teach children. Of course, the same children are taught, "Don't go into that neighborhood because They live there." If We are the world, where are They from? Maybe the idea is parenthetical: We (and They) Are the World.

Take the statement, "All men are created equal." You observe that damned They festering like a lesion on the milky skin of equality, and you hear the silent addendum: "But They shall be slaves."

From the beginning, individuals have fought the perpetrators of They with everything the world offered. Now people continue to batter, dissect, and analyze the problem with technologically advanced weapons. Oh sure, the problem of They may go into remission occasionally, but only for a little while. Given time, They springs forth once again and malignantly eats into the country.

The country thought the "They" curse was defeated in the sixties. Activists marched against it in Washington, D.C. Through a dosage of legislation, the government changed They into We. Congress passed new laws to enforce old ideals. When the They was thought to be quarantined forever, society hopefully lowered the dosage. Unfortunately, the caretakers of equality forgot about secondary infections.

Soon the infection surfaced again, this time in suburbia, the land of unlimited upward mobility. Suburbanites believed that the suburbs offered open spaces. But the move to the suburbs also occurred because They remained in the cities. Now, They were becoming upwardly mobile in the wrong places, so suburbanites revived the spirit of the Ku Klux Klan.

The ironic thing is that They sometimes become Us. Some of the original Theys spoke with a brogue, ate pasta, and celebrated Passover. The remaining Theys listen to soul music, eat black-eyed peas, and speak jive. Melting into Us, the old They finds itself equally susceptible to the new They.

The underlying problem is not in the old They or in the new They but in Us. The separation is arbitrary. The hopes, the dreams, and the ideals that we claim are the hopes, the dreams, and the ideals that they share. We cannot divide They from Us because They are Us. Our American Dream shares space with the ultimate American delusion: They.

Maybe after another 200 years the "They" curse will die once and for all and leave the country with a true We. The scars will remain, but maybe We will finally include everyone. But will We really be able to cure the blight of the Something that was lost? Remember the Puritan witch who cursed the Something of equality? Well, she still lives. The witch hates another Something: Their economic success.

The witch has filled the American pie with rotten apples. When They turn 18 and prepare to enjoy the pie, They find equality means a roach-infested apartment and economic success means a minimum-wage job. They wonder what happened to all the juicy apples.

When healthy and ripe, the apple, which may suggest both equality and economic success, is the pride of any owner. But as the rotten apple breaks open and brown mush oozes out between your fingers, the worm of prejudice is revealed at the core. Oh, the outside still looks okay. That's the danger of the rot; the core is hidden by a healthy exterior.

Cities were supposed to give Them a piece of the fresh apple pie. But, as utopian as cities seem on the outside, pick up a city to look closely; it, too, oozes out of your fingers. It's hard to pursue equality and success when you are weakened by starvation. Of course, you still have equality, as evidenced by your liberty to die from exposure or malnutrition.

Where did the country go wrong? We were supposed to be the land of the middle class. No very rich, no very poor. Like the rotten apple, however, the middle class seems to be dripping out of its skin. All that's left of the middle class is the sticky, mushy stuff that remains on your fingers, with the worm of prejudice resting there comfortably. We failed somewhere. Before, They would pursue happiness by reaching for the American Dream. Today, They have awakened and have discovered an American nightmare. They reach out and grab the Dream. Instead, They taste the sticky stuff of despair. The high-rise condo, the health club membership, the sleek sports car, and the pedigreed scottie have dripped out of the picture. A warm subway grate, a shopping bag, and restaurant refuse crawl out of the mush to replace the Dream. The rich get richer. The poor get poorer. And the scottie is shot for dinner.

Nobody is willing to share. We are content to keep the Somethings for Ourselves. But you can't separate the Somethings from the rest of the country. You see, the Somethings are for Everyone. Equality. Economic success. That's what America is all about. But the nation lost it. Somewhere.

Maybe the Somethings are still out there. Hiding. Ready to surge forth and take the first chance they have to embrace Everyone in America. Maybe.

Greg Jao

National Reactions—Conflicts

The greatest pressure for black students is that we must achieve athletically to be recognized. The only way we are recognized is if we make the winning touchdown or score the winning basket. This is discouraging to students who go unrecognized but achieve in other areas such as fine arts, industrial arts, and the sciences.

This system does have one good feature. . . . Because of athletics, some students are given the opportunity to go on to higher education. Even still, we recognize that many talented people go unnoticed. America must ask itself, where will the next Ron McNair, Jesse Jackson, and Shirley Chisholm come from? Will they come from the football field?

Camille Carson, 17
Bakersfield, California

I'm black, and I have a Puerto Rican boyfriend in Jacksonville, Florida. . . . Believe it or not, I think my boyfriend has more hurt and pain than any black person I've ever known. He tells me how guys have ganged up and knocked his books out of his hands because of his race. . . .

All he thinks about is going to New York, where he won't have to worry about people talking about his skin color or thinking that he is "one of a kind" and "as much of a troublemaker as the rest of them."

That's the same way it is with me. Though I get along with just about anybody and a lot of people, both white and black, think I'm charming, I know that the small technicality of being black will always make a difference. . . .

Sometimes I encounter prejudice toward another black person, usually one that doesn't look as fortunate as the rest of us. . . . Some people don't realize that we are all the same, whatever color we are. . . .

My boyfriend could pass for a white guy if he wanted to, but the way he talks gives him away. Maybe if we all were the same color and talked the same way, the world would be better.

Michelle Hutto, 18
Columbia, South Carolina

People around here are raised not really knowing anything about the different races except what they see on the TV or in the newspaper. I've noticed that if I'm with a group of people at an activity or sports event, people around me will comment on black participants, not knowing they're really putting them down.

I don't think that blacks yet have equal rights. It's been over 20 years since President Johnson signed the Civil Rights act, but I feel there is too much prejudice. . . .

People who haven't lived or been around people of different races feel

superior because. . .they don't know anyone of a different race.

Bryn Tejral, 17
Wahoo, Nebraska

Black-white relations at Hinsdale Central definitely need to be improved. There are only about ten blacks at this white suburban high school of Chicago, and many of them seem to be treated like all other students. However, those outside the Hinsdale area are treated with great prejudice.

I feel that what Central needs most of all is a magnet system. I attended Horton Watkins High School in suburban St. Louis (Ladue) during my first two years of secondary school. In Ladue, approximately 15 students were bused in from the city. . .to attend HWHS.

It is a popular, successful system they have there, and it has improved black-white relations greatly. Students, through this system, have found that blacks are not "that bad" after all and really much the same as everyone else. . . .

When white Chicago suburban students think of blacks, they think of the poor, homeless blacks in the city and their lives of crime and drugs. They stereotype these people as ones who will bring crime and drugs and poverty into the area, and the whites keep them out.

Surely, there is a way to combat this

type of stereotyping and prejudice. I feel it can be done with a lot of cooperation and effort of the communities of Hinsdale, Clarendon Hills, and Oak Brook as well as a magnet-type program to be used by Hinsdale Central High School.

Tom Ashworth, 17
Hinsdale, Illinois

I've been around many "friends" who talk about blacks as though they were inferior. . . . They say things like, "Blacks and whites shouldn't date—it would ruin their lives." They also comment that blacks "might as well all die off because they don't have a life."

It saddens and enrages me to know my so-called "friends" speak this way. I try to put myself in their shoes and think of excuses for them, but the solid truth is, there is no excuse.

I realize they were brought up that way, but if this continues so will their children. It's too bad to know that this kind of bigotry won't end with our generation.

Joy Russell, 16
Champaign, Illinois

I live in a very prejudiced community that has a very hard time accepting any blacks. The few at my school are often harassed. It is very difficult for them as there are just three in a school of 1,600. What can be done to improve relations? Sadly, I don't think very much in a community that's always been prejudiced. . . .

Because prejudice is a result of ignorance, the only real answer is education. But how can you teach an extremely prejudiced community not to be? We learn from our parents and elders who have already learned and taught us prejudice. . .in subtle ways—like not allowing us to go into the city, Detroit, where the black population is very high. I guess. . .that my community. . .is not likely to change soon.

Katy Boettcher, 17
Grosse Pointe Farms, Michigan

The acceptance of blacks is not the issue. What is the issue is the respect for blacks that people hold. Legally, society accepts minority populations. However, often minorities do not gain the respect of a society. They have the legal rights that are necessary but are still indirectly discriminated against. . . .

Although blacks have made great gains in this area, there are many people who do not respect blacks. . . . While these people may someday change their opinions, they cannot be forced to change. They can still hold their own opinions, regardless of what a law dictates. It will just take time for blacks to gain the respect of others, and that isn't even a guarantee.

Matt Hayek, 16
Iowa City, Iowa

The following appeared as letters to the editor in the Trapeze, the student newspaper of Oak Park-River Forest High School in Illinois.
This letter is not meant to offend anyone. I'm not racist or anything, but I think it has to be said. I believe that I speak for a lot of people. Ever since I was little, I heard in school about how Oak Park-River Forest was so much into integration. But we still don't have it. What we have, for the most part, is

white kids and black kids in the same school but no mixing. I don't know why this is, but it has some pretty bad effects.

The blacks tend to stay to themselves, like sitting in one big group at lunch or getting together in one big group before school. They don't even attempt to blend in. I don't believe they have to, but when you start complaining about not having blacks in Student Council or on Tau Gamma, it goes back to the fact that most black candidates aren't familiar with the white kids who vote.

Also, I've noticed that the black kids that do mix and don't submit to the "black image" in dress, attitude, behavior and friends aren't treated fairly by the other black kids.

Why should everyone in the cafeteria only listen to "black music" all lunch period? Why should special emphasis be put on a lot of people who don't want to be a part of the school. . .anyway?

Suburban kids have many stereotypes, . . .even though most kids aren't racists. Most of the black kids don't try to erase those stereotypes. They unknowingly reinforce them. You can't be equal in something if you're not willing to be a part of it. You can't hope to succeed in something you basically ridicule. Why can't blacks blend like the

Jews, Italians, and Irish did?

The government should help minorities, but they have realized that they must help themselves with their own social problems. There are important lessons that most minorities, like Asians, have learned, and they are doing good. It's time our black citizens and some of our black students do the same.

> *Student*
> *Oak Park-River Forest High School*

In reply to your question. . ."Why should everyone in the cafeteria only listen to 'black music' all lunch periods?" Well, Mr. Nameless, maybe it's in public demand. And, too, we do blend in with whites. I personally have plenty of white friends. So maybe if you looked a little harder, you wouldn't stereotype blacks.

> *Student*
> *Oak Park-River Forest High School*

I am one of many angry students who has read the preposterous article. I would like to say it's not just the blacks that stay in their groups but also whites. After all, "It takes two to tango." In other words, we cannot mix with whites if they don't mix with us.

And I resent the fact that the person who wrote this letter said, "The black kids that do mix and don't submit to the black image." What exactly is the "black image"?

It's kind of hard to believe that this person is trying to help with the problem of racism in our school. . . . Also, you mentioned that blacks aren't trying to erase those stereotypes. How in the hell are we supposed to erase those stereotypes when you keep reminding us about them.

> *Cynthie Matich*
> *Oak Park-River Forest High School*

Blacks don't need the government's help to solve our social problems. What we need is the attitude of Caucasians changed toward us.

Asians and other minorities have not experienced the same atrocities as blacks. They are more easily accepted into the mainstream than blacks. Considering historical situations of blacks, we have done quite well.

> *Pamela Yvonne Parks*
> *Oak Park-River Forest High School*

Although the letter. . .wasn't meant to offend anyone, it did.

It is true that Oak Park and River Forest hasn't been totally integrated, but it can't be solely blamed on the blacks in the school. Yes, blacks do tend to stay to themselves, but so do whites.

It seems to me that the problems with integration are being put off on the blacks when it takes a two-way effort to end segregation.

> *Sylene Isaac*
> *Oak Park-River Forest High School*

One race feels superior to another. . . whites feel that their race is superior because they look upon the blacks as weaker. This is why they took "blacks" from Africa to do slave work.

> *Paul A. Henderson, 14*
> *Los Angeles, California*

Discussion

Decatur, Georgia
Mount Carmel High School

What causes prejudice?

Mark: Black people are getting all the rights. More than whites. Every time something happens, they get into it. The whites don't have anything like the NAACP for protection if something happens to them. If a white cop shoots a black kid, the white cop gets kicked off the job. If the opposite happens, nothing ever goes wrong.

Robyn: We feel superior because the white men were here first, and the blacks were always treated as slaves. We had this idea in our head that they should be lower and the whites should be higher. They end up trying to fight for their rights, and that causes even more problems.

Tari: I resent blacks because I see a lot of them driving Mercedes down the road, and I am jealous of them. It should be me driving it instead of him because he's black.

Mark: You see them driving those cars. You turn around, and they're getting food stamps every week.

Tari: Blacks will always feel inferior because of their history, even if they do succeed in society. I don't think making them feel equal is necessary. They're leaving well enough alone for themselves. They're pushing hard enough to get their rights in society.

It seems like they should not hold high positions in society. I like the idea of them having a certain amount of black people in their jobs, but it should be a white person in control.

Neal: The media are getting better about portraying blacks. Long before, you'd see blacks, and they'd be maids or something. Nowadays you're seeing them come out even. Blacks have a type of charisma that whites don't. They're just more obnoxious. They're able to show humor better than white people.

I've been working at the mall. Black families will be real rambunctious, jumping all over everything, making a mess. White families come in, and they will have control of their kids.

Can blacks be accepted in a white society?

Neal: Eventually. If they move into an all-white school, it takes them a while to be accepted unless they're football players. One school has blacks on their team who are very good players. The other blacks are always being picked on.

Tari: The majority of black people who enter a predominantly white school will not be accepted. When a new black person walks in, the only person who is going to walk up to him and say anything is probably a black person.

It would be harder for the white person to be accepted by the black because blacks have such a different life-style. If a white person goes to a predominantly black school, that person is going to have to start acting like a black.

Is interracial marriage right?

Mark: I think it is wrong. When you have kids, they have to grow up and face the problem.

Dina: They're not white, and they're not black. They're in-between, and it's not fair to them.

Tari: The divorce rate would be a lot higher if they intermarried because their opinions and their life-styles are different. Except when a very high-class black person marries a white person.

How can society end prejudice?

Mark: I don't think you'll ever be able to do that. Prejudice keeps getting passed down through generations. As long as that keeps happening, you won't ever be able to get rid of it.

Neal: When people say something

obnoxious to you, you should ignore them. If a bunch of friends are trying to pick on somebody, you can say, "Hey, that ain't right." I'm not saying that would cure all problems between the races. I'm just saying that would help a little.

Boston
Madison Park High School in Roxbury

What causes prejudice?

Claire: People are jealous.

Marie: Another thing that makes a person prejudiced is if one person beats up another person. People say the whole race is that way.

India: People degrade blacks on TV most of the time. On commercials, you always see blacks cleaning. You always see the white people getting a new car or winning the lottery.

Aaron: Whenever something goes down, like a black person does something, the media will say, "a black youth." But when they talk about a white person, they will say, "John Doe was caught." They never say, "A white youth was caught."

Miles: Say your father is white and applies for a job. There's a black male, and he gets the job. The father may go home and say, "Well, that nigger beat me out." The child might think, "Yeah, that black..." It'll start building up tension, and the child will start hating blacks.

In our parents' time, they didn't have to work with other groups. Here at Madison, the yearbook staff has to work together. They don't have time to think, "He's white, and he's black." After a while, they look back and say, "Oh, he was a really nice person to work with." This changes their point of view.

How do people express prejudice?

Marie: One of my black friends came to South Boston. He didn't get too far because he almost got jumped. All I heard outside the windows was, "Nigger! We're

coming to kick your ass if you come back." One time I had to have a cop pick him up. The cop, who's white, got even more harassed for picking him up and driving us back.

How do students feel about busing?

Miles: It gives you the chance to meet other minorities and other cultures.

Marie: I've learned from it. No matter what minority you are, no matter what race or religion, you can learn something from somebody. That's what the school has taught me—to live with everybody.

How can blacks become socially accepted in the white community?

Aaron: They have to have lots of money.

Miles: You have to act white.

Marie: Kiss everybody's ass.

Claire: White people don't have a lot of trouble with black people as much as black people have trouble with white folks. Black folks are so much more understanding than white folks.

Marie: Whites have a lot more prejudice against blacks. Blacks, if you try to help them and to understand where they're coming from, will accept you.

Claire: Most black guys will go with a white girl, but most white guys will just look at you like, "Oh, no. I don't want to go with that nigger girl."

Miles: If I owned a business, I would go with black people because they are going to work because they are used to working. I would have some white people in there because they're helpful. I'd have a white secretary so she could organize and stuff.

Claire: When white folks get married, they figure, "I'm going to stay home, look after the kids, and my husband will look after me and feed me." Black people want to work.

Marie: The rich white people make everybody else do their work, just

Whites and Blacks 37

like they did with the slaves. But the slaves worked their asses off to get what they wanted. And to this day, I still believe that blacks work a lot harder to become what they've become than whites do.

Is interracial marriage right?

Aaron: Hey, if you fall in love with a white lady or a black lady, that's love. I'll marry her. As long as she loves me and I love her, we have the right to get married, no matter what color we are. I asked my father once, "Hey, what if I married a white lady?" And he said, "Hey, I'll beat you to the wedding." He won't have anything to do with me and her.

Gidget: But then, you go through with it and people start calling you Oreo cookie, or chocolate chip, and then that'll bring problems to your kids.

Aaron: Mixed couples have kids who are prettier than just two black people. Two black people or two white people will have ordinary kids, but mixed couples will have special kids. If a black person and a white person have a kid, the kid won't have to try to get a tan because he'll already have that nice golden complexion. They won't be using any cream to make them lighter because they're already light.

Marie: If a black and a white person love each other, it doesn't matter what other people think, but they're going to get all this crappola from people who don't think it's right. I like this black kid, and we do a lot of things together. But we also get ridiculed for it because I'm white and he's black. My mother's for it, and his mother's for it. But his friends are against it, and my friends are against it. The hell with everybody else.

I know these two people, and one's black and one's white, and they're married. Their daughter, who is light-skinned, gets ridiculed. The father who comes to pick her up, he's black. Everybody's like,

"Oh my God, her father's black!" They really do a job on her.

India: I know this girl, her mother's black and her father's white. She looks more white than anything. They all call her white, and she says, "Look, I'm not white, I'm me. I have black in me, and I have white in me." She really doesn't have too many problems with it.

How can teenagers overcome prejudice?

Miles: Each individual has to seek inside, sort it out, and get rid of it.

Aaron: I don't think you can do anything. Prejudice is here to stay. Everybody's grown up with it. White people have to teach their kids to love black people, and black people have to teach their kids to love white people.

Claire: I would try to get everybody together and talk to them. Show them it doesn't make any sense to go on fighting each other. If you come together and stay together, this world would be a better place.

Miles: Maybe you have to use witchcraft and wring it out of their souls.

Marie: The first thing people would have to do is respect the fact that people are different. I don't think it's going to happen in my lifetime. Maybe eventually, but it's going to take a lot of work and a lot of effort.

DAN O'BRIEN
LTHS.

How do students feel about busing?

Shawn: I had some friends when the buses first started coming over here. The blacks didn't like the whites, and the whites didn't like the blacks. They weren't used to being around each other.

Darrell: There were fights and riots. Destroying the school property. Vandalizing the buses. Breaking the windows of teachers' cars. Spray-painting the walls.

Yvette: When the westsiders had to catch the RTA, the eastsiders used to chase them to the bus stop. When the bus came, the westsiders still kept running because they were so scared they would be jumped.

JoAnn: A group of white boys were in the rapid station, and a group of black boys made them take off their tennis shoes. They were standing there in their socks. We were in the rapid station once, and they were throwing rocks.

Dawn: The faculty did things like seating everybody in alphabetical order. When we were running for student council, we had to have an even number of blacks and whites on our slate. They think it gets us together.

A lot of my family is very prejudiced. Busing was a total outrage to my parents. They discussed the possibilities of moving to a suburban school district.

JoAnn: There was a lot of protesting. The parents were out there. "No bus for us." I don't think there was a reason for that. When you go out into the world and get a job, you're going to have contact with blacks, whites, Puerto Ricans, Asians, and whatever. You have to get that experience. Once the students started coming to school, they had to live with it. All the picketing and everything didn't solve anything.

What broke the prejudice was that, if you're going to school with someone, you start listening to the same music that they do, get involved in the things they like, and go to the same parties. I don't think the prejudice was from the students. It was from the parents.

Dawn: My dad is very outspoken. If he sees a black, he makes his feelings known. He taught us that this was the way we were supposed to feel. I was so afraid of blacks when I went to junior high, it was terrible. But the more I got to know them, the more I discovered that they were afraid of me too.

How can teenagers end prejudice?

JoAnn: When the adults are old and we are adults, I think that's when prejudice will stop.

Shawn: Schools can educate people—like a black history class.

JoAnn: Have visitations. Suburban schools are not that far. They could have a field trip to West Tech and see how we get along. Or have special activities.

Shawn: I don't think prejudice will ever stop. It will be here until we all go away. You have to get used to it.

Gloria: It hurts you to know that you can't get along with one another. We have 22 different nationalities. Why must we fight?

How does teen prejudice compare with adult prejudice?

Kris: Adults are more set in their ways. They're like, "I'm 30 years old, and I haven't thought any different." Teenagers can see different views.

Brad: We've had experience with blacks and different minority groups, but our parents haven't. I don't think it's just because we are teenagers.

Sue: My parents used to live in Chicago when it turned all black, so they have this big prejudice against blacks. I've never lived in a place where there are all blacks, things are getting run-down, and there's more crime. So I don't have anything to base prejudices on, except for what my parents tell me. The experience I've had with black people has never been bad, but my parents have seen a lot more than I have.

Gerri Long (parent): They've also suffered an economic loss, in their minds. They had to move from a neighborhood that they really liked because they felt forced out. Today's teenagers are much more open. When I was a teenager, you just did not mix. I grew up in a white suburb, and you never mixed with anybody. The blacks lived in their own community. The whites lived in their own area. Today there is more of a chance to mix. Today's teenagers have learned that some of the myths that they have heard are not true.

Sue: But our society really isn't mixing. It's people who are mixing us with black people. It's not like the teenagers of today are reaching out to the black people. The blacks are more or less just coming in.

I work at a place where we've hired 84 blacks. I've seen good black people and bad black people, but I've also seen that they can be my friends.

Julio: You have to give everybody a chance. They are just other people. We don't have to refer to them as blacks, spics, or whites. Just all people.

How do teens learn prejudice?

Brad: The whites need to feel better than blacks, because they're different. It's a way to dismiss them as something less important. You either have to feel superior to them or understand them, and it is easier to feel superior to them.

Sue: Ever since I was young, my parents have always been totally prejudiced against black people. I met this guy at work, and he was black. He was very nice, and I was going to go out with him. My parents wouldn't let me get in the car with him. They passed that on to me. Until I met my first black person, I was conditioned not to like him.

Meaghan: Our parents grew up in the fifties when a lot of black people were moving forward and wanting to be equal. A lot of whites resented that.

Long: The blacks became competitors for their jobs.

Magnus Seng (parent): We had a lot of institutionalized prejudice in this country until Martin Luther King said, "To hell with this." The country changed.

We have prejudices that say, "You'd better lock up your cars in a black neighborhood. If you don't, they'll steal your tires." It also goes the other way around. If you are a black person, don't go to Cicero or, "Baby, don't go into a white neighborhood, or you're dead because those honkies will kill you."

There is a basis for the stereotypes in general statistics. There are poor neighborhoods in the city that have higher crime rates. Your property is in greater jeopardy. That may or may not be a function of color. I'm sure it isn't. In the 1930s Clifford Shaw did a study of delinquency. He found that delinquency stays in the same place, but the people move out.

The worst type of prejudice is when you don't know it's there. The subtle stuff. You go down South, and it's not too subtle. My neighbor is convinced that blacks are biologically inferior. He won't even admit that they are human. They are subhuman. That raises him.

Boston
English High School

Huston Crayton (social studies teacher): I live in Brockton, which is the cheapest suburban area. I find it more racist than Boston simply because the folks are where "white flight" started.

Whites were moving out of the city, and blacks were migrating in. Whites had middle income jobs and could afford to move out there to the suburbs. Now blacks can afford to go out there. There are a lot of strong feelings because the whole idea was to get out of the city away from the minorities.

Minorities are being given jobs in the fire department and as teachers because of affirmative action. They're being given jobs as policemen. Those salaries are $20,000 to $25,000, which means if the wife works in the post office and the husband is a teacher, they can move out to Brockton with their white-collar white brothers and sisters. When whites see that, they feel like they have their backs against the wall. "We tried to get away from that."

What causes racism?
Crayton: Students are so naive. They just see racial problems. I try to show them that the picture is who has and who hasn't. It's not necessarily the color. The poor white man is not better off than the poor black man. Blacks and whites ought to come together and lobby for things that will affect everybody.

The more money a person has, the less racist he is. I don't see too many doctors fighting about going to school with blacks. The most friction is usually from the poor people who are frustrated. Jobs have a lot to do with it. They're fighting over crumbs. They're fighting over jobs that pay well with a little bit of education. But there are only so many jobs like that. Years ago the Irish had all the public municipal jobs, and the Italians had all the construction jobs. The government says you have to share

them. And there are just not enough.

If I gave everybody in South Boston or Roxbury 40 grand, we'd have 80 percent of all the racial problems down the drain. Give everybody a decent living, no problem. Blacks would be able to drive around in South Boston, and everybody would be friends. If people are doing well, they tend to get less involved in this racial garbage.

Atlanta
the City Hall

John Lewis (U.S. Congressman, former leader of the Student Nonviolent Coordinating Committee): I was born and raised 50 miles from Montgomery [Alabama], the home of the modern civil rights movement. I was greatly inspired by what I saw happening. It was like a dream come true. I saw this young Baptist minister leading 50,000 people down the road to freedom.

At an early age, I saw the evil of the system of segregation. We were bused to school past the white school. We had the old buses, the broken down buses that had been left from the white schools. We had to use books that were left over. The message of Martin Luther King Jr., the message of love and nonviolence, provided a way to use our bodies as a tool of protest. You saw teachers, lawyers, doctors, and at the same time you saw maids and janitors, just everyday people, coming together to fight for what they believed in, in a nonviolent manner. They set in motion a nonviolent revolution.

We need legislation across the country to remove the remaining vestiges of segregation and racial discrimination. The scars and stains of racism are very deep in American society. We have to have laws on the books, but we have to make those laws real.

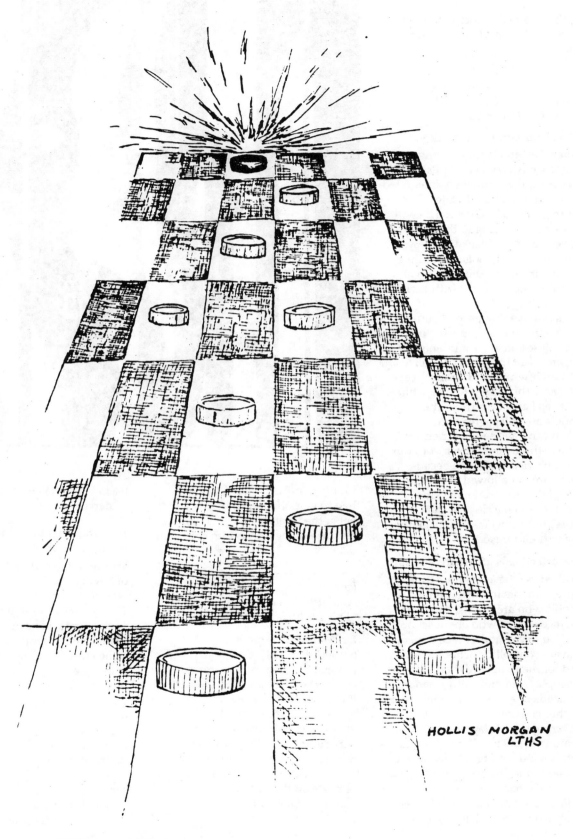

Whites and Blacks

We need to do more than open the door. We have to go that second mile.

Boston
Madison Park High School

How important is integration?
Robert Perkins (administrative assistant): Alabama and Mississippi have the most completely integrated schools in the United States. The South gave kids a choice. The white kids started moving to the black schools, and the black kids moved into the white schools. Once they mixed with each other in schools, they also began to mix with each other socially.

It's not like that here. If you stand around this building during lunch, you will see all black students in one area, but they don't socialize with their white or Hispanic peers. The same thing goes for the whites. As far as I am concerned, the schools are still segregated.

You can have a white friend who can live three blocks from you, but you can't visit his house because blacks are not allowed in that part of the neighborhood. I have kids whom I can take close to their house, but I can't take them all the way to their house.

How effective is affirmative action?
Perkins: You have nearly 70 percent of the students in Boston public schools who are blacks. You have one race of kids who are in school, and you have another race of people who are controlling school. It's very hard for me to believe that a group of people from one culture can meet the needs of a group of people from another culture.

During the big layoff, I maintained my job, but my friend who is white and taught for seven years did not. In seven years he had never gone back and received any additional education. In three years I had two master's degrees. I was

saying to myself, "Jesus Christ, I had to work harder than this guy to get at the level that I am." I had no remorse in regards to him being laid off.

Portland, Oregon
Administration office of the Portland Public Schools

Dr. Matthew Prophet (superintendent): One of the problems teenagers have, irrespective of whether they are black, white, brown, or red, is a lack of appreciation for each other. We are attempting to infuse into the curriculum something that gives them a sense of pride in who they are. I think we will see a heightening of pride on the part of many of our students. Our first task is to re-educate our teachers. They can't

teach what they don't believe or understand.

How important is it to have minority teachers?
Prophet: It gets back to the concept of having a kind of role model with whom youngsters can identify. Though we'd like to believe that youngsters will have positive role models, whether they are of the same ethnicity or not, it's a matter of fact that people identify with individuals who are of their own ethnicity. "If they can do it, I can do it."

This works both ways. It's just as important to have minority teachers in predominantly majority schools as it is to have majority teachers in predominantly minority schools. Our staffing in schools should clearly reflect the student makeup.

42

Life necessitates interlocution and interaction between all social classes. The deprivation is just as severe and just as damaging in schools that are 100 percent Caucasian as it is in schools that are 100 percent black. There are blacks who will say there is great power in separatism. I continue to push for a fully integrated society. To the extent that it is not at present, we really have problems. You either face minorities as a child in school or face them later in life when you have not been prepared to deal constructively with them.

There is an absence of more advanced math and science courses that is reflective of the socioeconomic status of the family. Mathematics, Engineering, and Science Achievement [MESA] is a program to encourage students, particularly the minority and lower socioeconomic kids, to take math and science classes in high school. We try at middle school level to expose kids to engineers, doctors, and IBM people. The idea is to help kids see the importance of math and science. We have parents pledge that their kids in high school will take first year, second year, third year, and fourth year math and science.

Boston
South Boston High School

How has the school attempted to desegregate?

Jim Poor (social studies department chair): When the federal court order came down, we had a cardinal who said that the Catholic schools will not be an escape hatch for those white children trying to escape the pains of desegregation. But sure enough, Catholic school enrollment went up about 60 percent.

The big losers are those white kids who fled. We're living in an integrated, multicultural society, and everyone living in it has to function in it. That's the name of the game. The parochial schools are a cop-out.

Desegregation is a very difficult problem because of historical racial divisions. People like to regard Boston as a cradle of liberty, but in reality Boston is a very provincial town where you have a white section, a black section, and a Hispanic section. The biggest solution is to get to know each other and to get along with each other. We treat kids fairly and equally, and over a period of time everybody's pretty well adjusted.

During the days of desegregation, we had one big black kid and one big white kid who were tough and who had a lot of race on their minds. One day we had a fight between these two kids. Later we got the kids together. Shortly, it was, "Hey, nice to meet you." Those kids went on to play football. It was the result of being together and being exposed to each other. They respected each other.

Compiled by Greg Jao

Solutions

White people say that interracial marriages are all punished by Satan, or some garbage like that. Some black groups don't fight for equality but for supremacy. To me, a black who believes in that is just as racist as any Nazi or Klansman. . . .

It is incredibly important for people to stop seeing whites or blacks or Indians or Orientals—just see people.

> Colleen Coover, 16
> Iowa City, Iowa

If blacks and whites want to be accepted with each other, it has to start when they are young. We can't really take the adults or even teenagers and totally change their views about people.

> Kathi Smith, 17
> Iowa City, Iowa

Whites have to realize that blacks are just the same. Even if they are different colors, they are all just people. . . .

Try and make friends with many

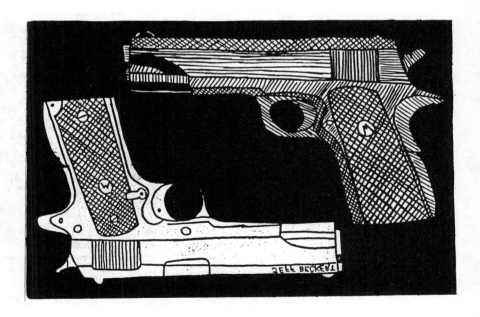

different people. You might learn more about yourself and other cultures. To be accepted by other people, just be yourself.

Jaya Gudimetla, 14
Irving, Texas

Race discrimination (the putting of one race over another) is a psychological problem. The "superior" race feels insecure with the "minority" race— probably out of fear of the "minority" race being stronger than the "superior" race. This was evident at the time I began taking swimming lessons. I had to take a test to determine what class I would be put in. I was a very good swimmer, but because of my race, I was placed in the lower group. . . .

I hope someday people will come together and affiliate no matter what the color or race.

Philip A. Henderson, 16
Los Angeles, California

If we had more black people in my school, the relations would be

better. . . . A boy. . .said, "They don't belong up here." Who's to decide whether or not colored people go to Wahlert High School?

Two colored people attend this school, and both are popular and seem content.

Stacey Jonll, 14
Dubuque, Iowa

Minorities would get along a lot better if they wouldn't treat themselves as minorities. They always have to group up and not mix in with others of a different race. The same would go for whites. We tend to group off and do not let those who try into our groups.

We should be very concerned about acceptance by another race because. . . we all live here together. If we want a group, let it be the human race, not the black race or the white race.

La Rae Eisenbise, 16
Albert Lea, Minnesota

My parents aren't prejudiced so I guess

that's why I'm not. But. . .an elderly lady that I work for. . .was complaining about how she didn't feel safe driving at night because of all the niggers that live in Oak Park. I was shocked when I heard her say the word "nigger."

I went home that night, and I thought about what she had said. Without blacks, we wouldn't have had Martin Luther King, Harriet Tubman, or even Michael Jackson. . . .

The exterior only holds the inside together. It's the inside that holds the feelings, the courage, the understanding, and the pain. People should think about the inside of people before they judge the whole person.

Elizabeth Hills, 18
River Forest, Illinois

Hinsdale could do a lot about improving the relationships between black and white people. . . . They could allow minority groups into the city. There are under ten black families in the whole area. There are about four blacks that go to my school.

A few years ago, a black family tried

to move into this town. They were treated very badly. They received threats; people vandalized their house; and they were evicted....

I have participated in a rally called "Stamp Out Racist Grafitti"...in downtown Chicago. At the last rally, we were attacked by Nazis. They had sharpened poles, clubs, and voo-doo dolls. They hurt many people, but the police did nothing to stop them.

Wendy Ohlendorf, 15
Westmont, Illinois

Black and white are colors that are total opposites. They tend to have positive and negative meanings that reflect our response to one another. Black usually signifies negative while white positive....

Throughout history there has been prejudice between both races that acts as a handicap as far as acceptance is concerned.... There tends to be a sense of fear about the two races becoming too involved in one another's traditions and coming to race for what it represents.

Another...gap between the two is ignorance of an individual's ideas and feelings.

The racial problem in our society isn't as evident but still exists; therefore, instead of denying that there is a problem it must be faced.

Neily Dickerson, 18
Los Angeles, California

People all over the world have a dilemma with black-white relationships. Three ways we can improve our relationships are to have social meetings, extracurricular activities, and Bible study.

These relationships can improve...by just showing feelings with each other and not judging them on just how they look. People are wonderful creatures. Everybody has at least one special quality about them, and it is important in a relationship to recognize that quality.

David Hittle, 16
Hinsdale, Illinois

Whites and Blacks

Chapter 3.

Anglos and Hispanics

"Nice shirt, I had one like that—last year." Jones's eyes flashed with the spiteful dagger of his words.

Last year? Hernandez brushed at his collar unconsciously. Hell, Jones still wore that shirt. He just said it to rip him down. Jones was always ready with a smart-ass remark. If it wasn't about his clothes, it was about his hair, his neighborhood, anything. I'm no different from them, Hernandez thought. I'm not a Mexican, I'm a Californian. I'm not a greaser, I'm a surfer. And I'm not a spic or a wetback. I'm not trying to fit in.

No, the name-calling had stopped now; that ended in grade school. Names, yelling, fights—every day, every hour, some reminder that he was different, different from them. Now the slurs were subtle: sly remarks, condescending smirks, awkward pauses. Skin color was just a starting block; the heavy artillery was their money, their cars, their all-American sun-tanned existence. And the ultimate weapon was their white, blue-eyed, blond-haired heritage. They knew Hernandez could never possess that heritage, and to them, maybe even to him, that made all the difference.

Yeah, a weapon to make him want what he didn't want, a weapon to confuse him. The Hispanics had enchiladas and refried beans, leather sandals, and the stuff his old man called cerveza that you drank with a lick of salt. The whites took it and warped it. They made what was foreign their own, made it a commodity in a boutique.

Was this what Hernandez wanted? Something beckoned in the glint of Ray-Bans, the beat of a new-wave station, the scent of Coppertone. The something was what they had in common, all of them, the class of '87. Was it just a style, an attitude? Hernandez tried to define it, but he knew he couldn't because he didn't have it.

Judi caught Hernandez' eye for a second when they passed in the hall. He didn't notice her. His smile was cute, no matter what her friends said.

"Oh, Gawd, he's a beaner!" Tiffany had snorted the day she mentioned it.

She wasn't going to ask him to the prom or anything. She had just mentioned his cute smile casually. Her friends were bigots, their bad jokes symptoms of real fear and disgust. Her friends complained about them "stealing jobs," but how could that be when their parents made $90,000 a year?

No, Judi thought, she wasn't going to ask Hernandez anything. She didn't know exactly why. Maybe her feelings had something to do with the man who did their lawn; the low-rider gangs in the east part of the city; or the guys who chased you in Tijuana, trying to sell lamps. She supposed she was a bigot, too. There were no Mexicans in the private schools. There were some here in public school, but they kept to themselves. They had Latino cars, Latino friends, Latino parties. Judi used to think that the whites and the Latinos were separate cliques. But when Tiffany called Hernandez a beaner, Judi began to wonder if clique was the right word. Maybe it was a massive rejection, a shutting out by whites.

On the way home, Judi detoured to check out a few streets leading to a Hispanic neighborhood. She swung around the corner, and there was Hernandez. He was wearing a gym shirt and had some books wrapped in another shirt, slung over his shoulder. He must have ripped it, Judi thought. Too bad, it was a nice shirt.

Eric Kammerer

National Reactions—Conflicts

Americans or whites seem to think that the whites are more important than any other person on the face of the earth. . . .

I can remember a time when I felt ashamed of the fact that I was Spanish-American. I would pray to God to please turn me white. I figured if I were white, then people would accept me into society.

Now, six years later, what other people think of me does not matter. . . . But what I think of them and their personalities matters more because if I don't like a person, it's not because of their color—it's because of what's in the inside.

Carol Juarez, 16
West Chicago, Illinois

Mexicans are expected. . .to be Americans' slaves and to take the worst of all conditions. . . .These people have earned this reputation because of the hateful attitude. . .that everything is theirs even though they are not citizens of the United States.

16-year-old female
Oklahoma

Prejudice against Mexicans is a lot different from blacks. It seems that prejudice toward blacks has decreased tremendously. . . .

We make fun of Mexicans because they can't speak English whereas blacks can. They are very smelly whereas blacks are not.

The Mexicans live in very cheap housing, drive very old and cheap Novas or Vegas. Blacks tend to be more expensive when it comes to that. We assume if we see a shitty Nova that is 15 years old that some Mexican probably owns it. We have prejudice against them for that.

Why can't these dirtbags learn to speak English and wash their oiled-down hair? Why do we have to adapt to see bilingual signs all over the place?

It would be nice some day not to see 27 Mexicans (beaners) squeezed into a piece of crap Vega and just be an eyesore to the town in which we live.

If you want to be rich in my town, first of all you can sell soap and deodorant to the spics, and of course, some shampoo. Find a homosexual spic and give all the Latin Kings [gang] AIDS. This way, all the rats in town would die because they would have no homes to live in.

17-year-old male
Illinois

Movies have encouraged whites to be prejudiced by the influence of actors, such as Al Pacino playing a Cuban cocaine dealer. "Miami Vice"— programs related to Hispanics in drugs.

Esther Rosales, 16
Portage, Indiana

Today there are 13,000 people living in my town, 40 percent spics.

All us American boys hate the Latin Kings because they think they're hot shit fighting people ten on one. They always have to travel together. If I ever get a hold of one of those damn spics, I will fucking, goddamn tear him limb from limb.

They hit on white underclass girls. They are dirty, smelly, and greasy.

There are about 100 black people living in my town. They are clean, cause no trouble, speak English, and are very nice. There is nothing wrong with blacks.

> *17-year-old male*
> *Illinois*

I don't think that there are as many groups such as the KKK that are against Hispanics. . . . In West Chicago, there are a few blacks but many Hispanics. . . . People treat the blacks well. When I'm in the locker room, I always hear stuff like, "I'm going to kick that spic's butt." Most people just call Hispanics names.

> *Scott Christiansen, 17*
> *West Chicago, Illinois*

Even though it shouldn't be this way and I'm ashamed to admit it, I find myself thinking thoughts of judgment about Hispanics whereas I wouldn't of blacks. When I think of blacks, no certain image comes to my mind because I know a lot of them. I realize that each one is different, just like whites.

But I do hesitate to get to know Mexicans. There are exceptions, of course. One of my closest guy friends is Mexican. But he's popular and socially accepted. I know him from the inside so I rarely ever look at the outside. It certainly doesn't stop me from being close friends with him. In fact, I don't even consider him Mexican.

A large percent of our school is Mexican, and there are very few blacks. Almost all the blacks fit into our social groups because they've worked their way in. When I think of most of the Mexicans in our school, I think of gangs and guys going around in cars being perverted. . . .

> *17-year-old female*
> *Illinois*

Whenever I go somewhere with my Mexican friends, people look at me as if to say, "Why are you with them? You're better than they are. . . ."

I was in the store with some of my friends, and a salesperson came up to me. I told this person that I didn't need any help, but when my Mexican friend asked for some help, the person looked at her and said that she could find whatever she wanted by herself. . . .

Recently in our school, one of my friends was suspended for wearing black and gold. The next day almost everyone wore black and gold, but the only ones they called down to the office were the Mexicans. . .even though the white people were wearing black and gold.

> *Sheryl Wilmer, 18*
> *West Chicago, Illinois*

Discussion

Prejudice

Tucson, Arizona
A local high school

Queta: A lot of the focus on the Hispanic community has been negative, especially when they speak of the illegal aliens. They think a person is Mexican just because he speaks Spanish. They always say that we take jobs away from the Americans.

Poli: And crime. It's up to Hispanics to change those views. They have to help themselves to get along in the world.

Vangilia: It's like a school reputation. Once you've got it, you'll always have it. In order for you to change it, you've all got to get together and change it. I don't think it will ever happen though.

Poli: It's going to take a long time to abolish prejudice and to get Hispanics not to feel part of a second class. Eventually it's going to happen. With all of the new

programs, there are going to be role models and more Hispanic people in prestigious jobs. That will help the Hispanics move up.

The biggest prejudice that Hispanics have toward whites is that all white people think they're better than Hispanics. Most older Hispanic people don't trust white people because they always think they're going to get screwed over. That hurts because those opinions go down to their kids and it's really hard to change.

Queta: When there is an Anglo around, we'll speak Spanish as kind of a put-down. We know they won't understand it. Or we'll just call them names like gringos or galachos. The Hispanics are a resentful culture. They are tired of being called a minority because many times they are the majority—like in Tucson.

They see whites as successful people, but whites are also so silly at times. They have no values, no traditions, so they're an easy mark for jokes. Whites don't understand the jokes.

Poli: I think interaction between whites and Hispanics would change prejudices. Being exposed to different people can help. Try to take as much information from them as possible. All the races want to isolate themselves. They don't want to see different cultures.

Gary: They have to unite and go to the government so a change can be made nationally. Until then, whites will be on top, and minorities will be on the bottom.

Queta: There was a time when many young Hispanics were getting into gangs because they felt like they were isolated. That was a prejudice in itself because either you were a Mexican or you were a *tola*, a gang member. In reality, the *tola* could be a football star or an honor society student.

Poli: If anything bad is going to

happen in Tucson, it's going to happen here in South Tucson. Trichloroethylene soaked through the ground to the water supply. They think TC causes cancer. There's been a lot of cancer in my family, and there never was before. There are problems with babies on this side of town.

As long as it doesn't bother any other part of Tucson, they don't care. They are not going to take as much time to fix things up for minorities—Hispanics and blacks—because they say if they make something nice here, Mexicans don't care. The Mexicans are going to mess it all up and write graffiti on it.

I don't think job quotas really help that much. As a Hispanic, I don't want someone to hand me a job. I want to be hired because I can do it well, not because they need three Mexicans and two blacks. That's robbing me of my pride.

Queta: I know of a case where a man didn't get accepted to a university because they had to fill a quota of minorities. Even if minorities had lower test scores, they would get in. I don't think acceptance should be based on quotas. Acceptance should be based on whether you qualify. Quotas make us look bad.

Is there pressure to conform to American life?

Queta: I never felt that I had to become more Americanized. I felt encouraged not to become Americanized because it would take so much away from me. In the mid-seventies if you were Hispanic you hid the fact. You disguised your ancestry.

Now if you're Mexican, people say, "Hey, that's great. You're the up-and-coming minority group. You're going for everything." I don't think kids say, "I'll stay out of the sun so my skin lightens. I'll bleach my hair blond."

Poli: Hispanics can try to be as white as possible and try to fit in, but they never will. By trying to fit in, they're alienating themselves. I think it's a waste. They will always be different.

You have to realize who you are and accept that you're Hispanic. You can't get rid of your culture. You have to be proud of it and make peace with yourself. Then you can do whatever you want. They can't put you down for what you are.

Chicago
Casa Aztlan (community youth center)

What prejudices affect Hispanics?

Sandra: In certain neighborhoods I feel that people are looking at me and saying, "What are you doing here?" I'm afraid of the blacks who move into this area.

Sal: Each race is prejudiced against the other. If you are prejudiced against me, I don't care. God put us here together. We have to expand in order to change our thoughts. If I don't know how a white person is or how a black person is, I'm probably going to be hateful to them.

There is prejudice in the Hispanic community because you have the Chicanos who are prejudiced against the full-blooded Mexicans. They think we came to this country illegally. I have my papers, but I'm not ashamed to say that I'm Mexican. The Chicanos say, "I'm not Mexican. I was born here. I'm American."

Rodney: I always was prejudiced against native Mexicans until I realized that my family would have been considered brazers or wetbacks at one time, too. But I'm third generation so I didn't think about it as my family.

Sonja: I'm prejudiced against blacks and Puerto Ricans. They are different from Mexicans. They talk faster. They are half black. At our

high school, blacks were the only group that I had trouble with. The whites have never bothered me.

What is the Hispanic view of the U.S.?

Sal: A majority of people come over here because it is the "Land of Opportunities." But that doesn't exist. Mexicans leave their country, and they suffer in the process of coming here or living here. When they came from Mexico, they had all these hopes: "Oh, we're going to become rich, and we're going to come back to Mexico, and we're going to have this and that."

In Mexico my family was rich, but when we came here, we were poor. Being around this neighborhood is very depressing because of all the poverty and the ignorance. Some Hispanic parents can't understand their kids. When parents tell them to do something, the kids just swear back. There are no chances to better ourselves.

How do whites view Hispanics?

Ernesto: They accept us better than blacks accept Hispanics.

Sal: It depends on which whites you are talking about. I have a lot of white friends who love my culture so I share it with them. But if people are in higher society, it doesn't matter what race you are because they don't want any part of you.

Rodrigo: Around where I live, the whites don't say anything to us. They just leave everyone alone. They don't start trouble. They just keep to themselves.

Rodney: White is white, and they will always be superior to us. They will always downplay us.

Sandra: It's not like the U.S. doesn't need any more people. History says all the people came over here and enriched their lives. Why should it be any different now than it was then? If people think there is a chance here, why can't they come in without the hassle and without being deported?

Gerardo: There are certain white people who say, "You don't belong

DAN O'BRIEN
LTHS

in this country." It's almost like gangs who say that a certain territory belongs to them. It's not their country either. Their parents were immigrants at one time, too. That's what is so unique about America.

Language barrier

Tucson, Arizona

Poli: It's the responsibility of all Hispanics to learn English and to learn it well. But they should never lose Spanish because that's something they have on everyone else. They have variety in culture and another language. Speaking both languages is priceless.

Queta: It's up to the students. They should want to learn English. You need it to get along in this country. It's not feasible, though, that English should be our official language in this country.

Poli: If you're planning to survive in the United States, you have to learn English. Every other country has an official language. The U.S. shouldn't be any different. People think that Hispanics can't do as well in English. They can't write as well or use grammar as well. That really bothers me.

Chicago

Sal: I don't think the government should change the street signs to include Spanish to make it easier for the people. When you make it easier, they become lazier. They're not going to have the hunger for knowledge. We need to communicate through the English language.

What causes the high Hispanic dropout rate?

Dionne: Either guys get caught up in gangs, or the girls get pregnant.

Gerardo: Or just the pressures in the school make them feel like they don't belong.

Rodney: The major reason for the dropouts is not a lack of intelligence, but it's the pressures. We have the talent.

Jesus: Your friends want you to party. If you are not like them, they call you something. You are afraid to be different.

San Francisco
Pacific News Service

Irma Herrera (journalist/attorney): I think there is a perception in American society that anyone who speaks a language other than English is not a real American. Even though many Latinos have been here for many generations, there's always a question about whether we have a right to be here because we look different and because we speak another language. So we have to defend our right to be here. And that's very uncomfortable.

Latinos are very tied to the Spanish language. White people say, "Why don't you learn English?" Well, we do learn English. The difference is we retain our language. And that bothers Americans.

Another difference between other immigrant groups and Hispanics is that the U.S. shares a 3,000 mile border with the Spanish-speaking world. When the Irish came and the Italians came, at some point there was a cutoff.

If you are a minority, such as a black or a Chicano, and you fail in school, people don't just look at it as your individual failure. They tend to attribute that characteristic to others. You don't have the right to screw up. Whereas if a white kid screws up, it's just, "Jack screwed up," or, "Mary screwed up." People don't say, "Oh man, all white students are dumb." But that happens to minority students.

The schools are also set up to treat you differently. A lot of kids who grow up in low-income neighborhoods are not being prepared for college study.

A lot of it is economic. How can your parents expect you to go to college when they need you to work after school to supplement the family income? They'd like you to go to college, but they know they can't help you out for four or eight years while you prepare for a career.

I'm very supportive of bilingual education. I don't think kids can learn if they don't understand the medium of expression. For example, it you take deaf children and speak to them in English, but haven't taught them sign language or lipreading, are you really educating them? No. Every bilingual program has English language structured into it. You should have several periods a day when you are having intensive language learning.

Today we don't have a melting pot. We have people who retain differences. We are beginning to accept that. We can have people who look different and who are still Americans and who can mix and match.

Family values

Tucson, Arizona

Francisco: I think Hispanic families are more united. The white people are more independent. When white kids turn 18, they want to leave the house.

Poli: In the American culture, it seems like you're supposed to do everything against your parents. Like in the movies, it's just "rebel." You've got to do the opposite of what they want. Many times rebellion is more harmful to you because parents have gone through the same stuff—you need them to guide you.

Vangilia: Hispanic families are more of a unit because we tend to see each other more. We're not like

Anglos, who say, "Well, I'll see you at Christmas time and maybe one week over the summer." Hispanics keep going back to the city they came from and keep in touch with their aunts, uncles, grandparents, and cousins. Many of them live in the same city or same area.

Poli: My parents create a stable environment at home. I don't have to worry about family problems. They help me, and I can just worry about school. I don't have to worry whether we are going to have food. That's taken care of.

Queta: I think Hispanics should be more flexible. If we have family problems, we are too proud to go to a counselor. It could be tearing the family apart on the inside, but it doesn't show on the outside. They're also not too crazy about letting their kids date. When kids turn 16 and want to go out, parents say, "Maybe you'll go out when you're 21." We're in an Anglo culture where people go out very young, but our parents can't see that. They want you to go out with a chaperone. They say, "Why can't it be like when I was brought up?"

Lombard, Illinois
Glenbard East High School

Walt: Family is important in Spanish culture. We're the type of family that sees the parents and grandparents at least every weekend.

Julio: Also, the grandparents may be living with you. The aunt and uncle are at home.

Walt: When we lived in Puerto Rico, we all lived in the same apartment. It was large, and it accommodated all of us—my grandparents, their seven kids, and whatever grandchildren were around. It was a five-bedroom apartment. When we came here, we had to see the family. If I don't see the family for two or three weeks at a time, I'm

almost crazy. "Who's done this? Who's done that?" I can't wait until Sunday to see the whole family.

Magnus Seng (parent): The Hispanics are from a world that is not as fast-paced or advanced as ours, and they have more time to become closer with their relatives. But we just don't have time for that sort of thing.

Walt: I think religion is really important in our culture, especially in our family. Most of our celebrations have to do with religion. Whenever we get together, it's because of a religious occasion. Our parents try to get us into the religion.

Julio: It seems like the "newer generation" Hispanics are not as involved with religion as their parents were. Some grandparents pray all the time and light candles all over the house. My parents are like that.

Walt: My parents felt that the United States was a place where they could succeed—"A Land of Opportunity" and a lot of possibility and prosperity. On one hand, it makes me feel really bad that Hispanics can't be accepted. Maybe they can add a lot to the culture, whether they're illegal or not. It's unfortunate that some people have to come here illegally, but they shouldn't be stigmatized just because of it.

Tucson, Arizona
A law office

Richard Gonzalez (attorney): What educators say about parents pushing their kids in a certain direction was very true in my case. My folks did not graduate from high school or have a college background. My father's philosophy is, "So long as you are always willing to work, you will have a job." He grew up in Texas where Hispanics were not allowed to go to certain schools. He didn't go to high school. When he

came to Tucson with the military, one of the primary reasons was so that his kids could go to school. I remember him saying, someday, if we worked hard and really wanted it, we could go to school at the University of Arizona.

They never pushed me to be a lawyer, but it was always understood that I would go to college, at least for my first year. If I didn't like it, they would let me walk away from it, but only after I had had a taste of it. In my senior year of high school, I went down to the recruiting center because most Hispanics join the Marines. I really wanted to join, but I knew I would disappoint my parents. I was going to be the first one in the family to graduate from high school.

At family discussions we would talk about right and wrong and getting into trouble. We would talk about what happens to people if they break the law, going to prison, and the implications of that. We talked about being a family unit. When one suffered, we all suffered.

Ties to Mexico

Tucson, Arizona

Poli: If you go back to Mexico, it's never the same. They'll call you a gringo or white. You're not accepted.

Vangilia: They ditch you because you ditched them. You left their race.

Poli: It's double jeopardy because if you come to the United States, you're a minority. If you go back, you're still not accepted.

Queta: The expectations for children are different. If I had stayed in Mexico, I would have been a secretary. But here my mother expects me to go off to college and do the best that I can. That's how it should be. Some Hispanics are prejudiced about the Mexicans who have been in the U.S. longer.

Chicago

Sal: I can't think of moving back there because I'm so used to the United States. I speak fluent Spanish, but there are some words that I don't know. I wasn't born here, but I have to stay here because I wouldn't know how to survive in Mexico.

Ernesto: When you live here for a long time, you start losing your culture. If you had to go back to Mexico, you would feel weird. When your parents want to go back, they don't understand why you want to stay here.

Sal: It's like the beat of the drum always stays in me. Even though I don't live in Mexican ways, I always am myself. But we had to break away from the culture to survive.

Ernesto: The Mexicans want to come here to learn the language and get into politics. They think everything is so easy.

Rodney: There's that big misconception that we have everything because we are in the United States. They don't know all the harassment, the prejudice, and the racism that we face. They have no perception of what we're going through here or how we feel.

Carlos: But, as each generation goes on, people will get better educated.

Gerardo: I'd rather see the government educating people to better understand each other instead of building nuclear weapons.

Sandra: They could have more organizations like Casa Aztlan to teach the Hispanic kids skills they can use in the future.

Rodney: The standards of living are high here. The only way we can change things is with our votes—to get people elected who are more responsive to our communities' needs.

Sal: The communities where few people vote never get their streets fixed or cleaned up. The "Little Village" is where most of the votes came from so their streets got fixed. But here in the Pilsen area, we didn't have many votes so that's why the streets are all torn up.

Jesus: If we gave up every time someone put us down, we would never go anywhere. It is slow going, but we are getting higher and higher.

Compiled by Gina Nolan

CHRISTINA SZYDLOWSKI
LTHS

KEVIN JOHNSON LTHS

56

Solutions

The biggest problem that Americans face today is the fact that the immigrants can't speak the English language. English is our language, and it is rapidly going out of style. . . . If we allow the immigrants to take over and speak their language fluently, we won't have a chance to keep English as our Number One language.

It's important to keep everything alive in America. It's the way we have been brought up.

> Thea L. Walker, 18
> Grosse Pointe Farms, Michigan

I thought when I was younger (at that time I lived in a mixed neighborhood) . . . . that everybody was equal. As I grew older. . . I saw how life really is between the whites and other colors. If you are white, you are accepted anywhere.

> Marianne Beal, 15
> Portage, Indiana

The Hispanics and Asians must have a strong urge. . .to learn a new language so that they would no longer be social outcasts in America. . . .On the part of America, the U.S. government should provide night schools in which these foreigners can learn to live in a society in which the customs are so different from their own. Without this government aid, these people will get nowhere.

> Lynda Rayos, 16
> Grosse Point Woods, Michigan

Prejudice toward Hispanics is a little similar to prejudice toward blacks. As a Hispanic, I don't experience this kind of problem because I usually am not around my people. Most of my friends are American.

I know that people act towards Hispanics in a bad way because a lot of Hispanics. . .act in a way in which they give themselves a bad reputation. . . .

I also know that a lot of Hispanics are real nice people. . .but once they move to the United States, they become like the others. Why? Because they have nobody else to be around because they don't speak English. But if they knew how to speak English, they wouldn't really want to be doing anything bad. . . .

I know a lot of Hispanics who want to try and be somebody in this country, but nobody gives them the opportunity to be that somebody. It is just impossible for them to get anywhere. They look for jobs, and employers look at their faces, or their names, and see that they look . . .Hispanic. They turn them down.

> Jorge Zamora, 18
> West Chicago, Illinois

My family was prejudiced against Hispanic people, but they have now realized that Hispanics are not different from anyone else in the United States. My closest friend is Hispanic, and she is the most caring and intelligent person I know, which proves to me that Hispanics are just like everyone else.

> Heather Harwood, 15
> Portage, Indiana

Hispanic children in America should be taught bilingually. Otherwise it is a shock for them to go from a Spanish-speaking home into an English school where they are punished for communicating in their native language.

> Caity Hellenga, 15
> Galesburg, Illinois

Chapter 4.

Majorities and Minorities

It's a bizarre day in Somewhereville, USA. As Mark and Carol step out of their house onto the street, they begin noticing subtle differences, not so much the triangular houses or the fishy odor in the air as the gray-skinned man wearing a tuxedo and walking a matching penguin.

"What the hell?" Mark manages to say as he stares in amazement.

"What's going on?" Carol asks.

"I . . . don't know. Let's ask someone."

They approach the man with the penguin. "Excuse me, sir," Mark mumbles.

No reply.

"Excuse me."

This time the man, with an expression of confused contempt on his face, turns toward them. "Xtaxtacbchal," Mark and Carol hear the man say. "Neewony urbleplot paw paw paw." The last words are spoken in a tone of utter disgust as the man walks off. Like stray puppies, Mark and Carol follow the strange man to a bus stop. The three wait in silence for the approaching bus. Mark and Carol follow the man onto the bus.

They seat themselves up front next to the door.

"Xacytqint!" the driver barks, pointing a bony finger to the rear of the bus. "Xacytqint, zunth!" he repeats gruffly. The driver's icy glare pins them to their seats with fear.

"What does he want?" Carol whimpers.

"I don't know," Mark answers, locked in a stare of morbid fear with the large man.

From the middle of the bus a harried, middle-aged woman yells out, "Qyick ex, nup shiz!"

A burly man storms up to Mark and Carol, wraps his callous gray hands around their necks, picks them up, and carries them to the back of the bus. A section of the bus, devoid of seats or handrails, is filled with penguins owned by many of the commuters. Here, Mark and Carol are left to spend the rest of their ride.

They bounce around among mounds of penguin feathers and feces for several minutes until the bus stops and they are able to get off. Mark and Carol wander aimlessly about Somewhereville looking for a kind face, someone who will explain what has happened to them. All they receive from people on the streets are looks of disgust.

It is about dinner time, and they are starving. They soon find what appears to be a restaurant. Mark goes in alone. He can't understand the language but the word *poseidon* keeps coming up. At least the people aren't contemptuous; in fact, they don't seem to notice him. Mark catches a glimpse of a platter of food on a table: to his horror, he sees an uncooked fish slit open from chin to tail. Slimy entrails droop from the carcass. Mark sprints wildly out of the restaurant.

"Carol, we've got to get out of here."

"What? Why?"

"I don't think we're going to have dinner here tonight," Mark says, and he recounts what he saw in the restaurant.

Eventually the pair stumble into a residential area where they meet a lady wearing a veil. She, by some miracle, speaks English and offers them dinner at her house.

"You wouldn't happen to have a hamburger, would you?" Mark asks.

"A ham what? No. Sorry."

"How about a ham sandwich?"

"Sorry, our religion prevents us from eating pork. I'll fix you a nice meal."

Carol and Mark stare at each other in horror. Their minds fill with images of fried monkey brains, goose feet pate in white wine sauce, and other dishes that might be considered "nice." Instead, the lady gives them a few hard, circular rolls as an appetizer. After a while, she dishes out a thick pasty fish dinner.

After thanking the lady for dinner, Mark and Carol begin the long trek home. The streets are empty, and their trip is uneventful until they meet Mike, an old friend they haven't seen since he moved to a different section of Somewhereville three years ago.

"Hi, Mike," Carol says.

"Xxxycchactlyl?"

"What? Remember us, Mike?" Mark asks after recovering from the initial shock of Mike's outburst.

"Only close friends and family may call me Mike, mister and miss."

"Sorry...uh...sir," Mark says.

"Xxyplecyl paw paw," Mike mutters as he walks away.

Mark and Carol continue on their way, and make it home with no further mishaps. Opening the front door, they both breathe a sigh of relief when they see their mother, unchanged from when they had seen her last. "I have some wonderful news for you. Remember your friend Mike? Well, his whole family is staying here for the week. They even brought their pet penguin!"

Dave Seng and Douglas Addison

MATTHEW HYDE
LTHS

National Reactions—Conflicts

As a minority myself from Vietnam, I know of many pressures I have to deal with in everyday life. People treat you differently because of the way you look or where you came from. . . .You try out for a team. You know you are as good as all the others. But the coach doesn't pick you because you look different from all the other people. It gets you so mad when this happens.

> *Hau Nguyen, 14*
> *Galesburg, Illinois*

Many Americans feel superior to the Hmong community because the Hmong get federal aid. When one sees a member of the Hmong driving a new car, there is resentment felt. Federal aid should be given to those Americans living in poverty.

> *Kellie Griffin, 16*
> *Stockton, California*

I don't really feel any racial pressure. . . because my town is a predominantly white neighborhood. However, I know that other races have to put up with a lot of crap just because they are a different color.

I admit that I am prejudiced. How? My friends and I often make fun of spics, Hindus, etc. If you are not prejudiced, you're only lying because everyone is prejudiced against someone or something. This is bad because. . . Spanish or black people have barely any chance of getting a job against a white person. . . .

I kind of feel like all those black movements for equality didn't work. You see, I work at a place where they have equal opportunity employment. . .but the black people who work there always get sent to do the dirty jobs, and the white people get the glory ones.

I personally would like to see all this bigotry stopped, but I don't see any way to make people change the way they think. Maybe if they put the bigoted people into a place where they are a minority, they would change their ways.

17-year-old male
Illinois

One of the major pressures that minorities face is the pressure to conform to the standards and ways of the majority. Many minorities find this to be undesirable simply because they are proud of their heritage and are comfortable with their way of life. This leads to additional pressure to have their ways accepted and understood.

Another major pressure that minorities face comes from having to overcome the stereotypes associated with specific groups. A lot of minorities grow up hostile and defensive simply because they are usually the first to be suspected of wrongdoing. . . .

In some ways there are even pressures to uphold some of the stereotypes of minorities. This probably stems somewhat from doing what is traditionally acceptable in their communities as well as upholding the pride of their different groups. . . .

I feel that one of the major pressures which majorities face is to stay separate and maintain their dominant position in our society.

Jacqie Neal, 18
Waverly, Nebraska

People who condemn minorities because they are different must remember that once one of their ancestors was an outsider to this country and possibly harassed in the same manner. This country was founded as a haven from persecution, and it is sad that we have debased our country to the levels of those from which our ancestors came . . . to escape.

In an ideal society, minorities should not have to change or conform at all. The unique traditions and special aspects of each minority could be preserved and enjoyed. Unfortunately, in our society before many of the minorities were diluted from exposure, the purity of the minorities only served to promote xenophobia and isolation.

Hopefully, there should be some way of preserving and working together—cooperation and individuality. The direction our society seems to be headed is a uniform people, an easy-functioning society without the problems of prejudice and without the opportunity for growth.

Maura Capaul, 15
Chicago, Illinois

The minority does not necessarily want control, but since it became a minority because of some difference, be it political, moral, or even physical, the odds are that eventually it will take its shot at the top. It must therefore have the patience it takes to wait for its turn at leadership.

The majority also has its short-comings. Being the side with the power, it must always appear not to be persecuting the minority. . . . History has shown that the majority often is not correct. If you could have told voters in 1972 that Richard Nixon was a crook, he probably wouldn't have been elected.

Jason Wheat, 17
Bakersfield, California

Tell them all to learn the language or go home. After all, it's their problem, not ours.

Ray Shook, 16
Oklahoma City, Oklahoma

America is supposed to be the great melting pot, but I think that's a wrong idea. Why live next to Joe Shmoe and wife who are just like everyone else in town?

I like to walk into a small store and meet someone who has a different type of life; it makes my life much more interesting.

In Wheeling, there is a new Canton food place. The man who owns it is the most friendly person. As I go in there often, we speak to each other a lot. He's told me about why he opened his shop. He's also told me a little about his language. I think more people like him would make America more interesting.

The only disadvantage is when the immigrant refuses to learn any English and can't communicate with us. That makes things so hard. . . . But people who are willing to learn make meeting experiences much more enjoyable.

Yvonne Farrow, 16
Prospect Heights, Illinois

Hispanics and Asians can and must overcome language barriers in order to live in the United States. American English is our national language, and it is not right for native-born Americans to be subjected to know Spanish or Asian languages in order to communicate with these immigrants.

Our parents and grandparents who immigrated to this country from Europe had to learn our language in order to become a part of the American society. Many have built up prominent businesses and even political careers. These people were proud to accept their new way of life and language that was an essential part of it. . . .

Many places in California, New York, and Florida . . . are bilingual. How can these areas allow themselves to be manipulated into learning a second language for survival? If these immigrants are willing to remain and take advantage of our country's wealth, why shouldn't they be forced to learn our language and our way of life?

Maria Bahanovich, 17
Grosse Pointe Woods, Michigan

Minorities should not have to change to be more like society. In fact, there should be no such thing as a minority. People

from minorities help our society just as much as anyone else. Minority groups contribute as much as other groups and make our society work.

Jean Boyd, 15
Paramount, California

Solutions

As a member of the Filipino community, I have seen drastic changes in the attitudes and personal views of the minority groups today. Everyone has followed the trend of becoming more and more American—so American that quite a few teenage minorities have dyed their hair blond and have prescriptions for hazel and blue contact lenses. In this respect, I fear that minority groups have or will lose perspective of their culture and their native background.

It is a privilege to be American, but people must not lose sight of their origins. . . . The Japanese should continue to eat sushi and wear kimonos even though they have developed teriyaki burgers and manufactured Cyndi Lauper clothes in Tokyo. Every culture has something to be proud of. They should exude this pride because it is twice the honor to be a part of two cultures.

Ronela Ferrer, 18
San Francisco, California

Through understanding, willingness, and patience, the language barrier can be broken. There are many programs that offer courses especially designed for foreigners . . . that teach the English language.

However, I don't think the responsibility of communication lies completely with "the other guy." Americans need to be educated too.

I think that children should be required to take a second language in school from grade school on. The benefits of knowing a second language are great and make communication in America's "melting pot" much easier.

Lynn Buzza, 16
Stevens Point, Wisconsin

Minorities are just as capable of succeeding as any other person. Sometimes they are more capable because they have to work twice as hard as everyone else to break free from the old established stereotypes. If there is any doubt as to this, one has simply to look at such successful individuals as Bill Cosby or Lionel Richie, for these men have reached a degree of success that few of those who condemn minorities will ever reach.

Therefore, minorities should not have to change. Their traits, like the traits of all others in America, are the ones that make our country the great country which it is today.

Troy Neil Stemen, 17
Van Wert, Ohio

Minorities should not conform to the fullest extent to the American society because they need to retain some traditions which identify them as the minorities. The U.S.A. is known as the "Great Melting Pot." Along with the different nationalities, the people bring different traditions. Who is to say exactly what social rules are the makeup of American society?

Betty Chan, 16
San Francisco, California

I myself belong to a minority, Koreans. I get most of the pressure from my parents. That's because they moved over here for my sake. They want me to do well in school and to have a social life, and I feel that I owe it to them since they sacrificed a much easier life for themselves in Korea.

The pressure I get from them are things like getting A's in school, joining sports, not drinking, not partying, and trying to be like the all-American boy next door. It can get worse sometimes because they put religious pressures on me also.

Another pressure that I have is trying to uphold a good image so people will respect me and my country. That

can be hard at times since I'm only human, and I get into as much trouble as everybody else.

My parents also pressure me to study a lot. They made me start studying for my SATs as a freshman, but I had two more years to take the tests yet. My parents also want me to do well in school so people will respect my nationality.

Another pressure is trying to remember my native language. But that's hard for me since I have lived in America since I was three years old. And it seems like people expect you to know your language, but they don't understand why you don't, which can get me very angry at times. They don't understand how hard it is to keep up with your own language when the people that you talk to the most speak English.

Also, people can't understand the prejudice that I have felt from other people, and that pressures me to try even harder at everything I do.

Byung Kang, 15
Mount Prospect, Illinois

Discussion

Olympia, Washington
Evergreen State College Summer Journalism Workshop

Jennifer (Seattle): I feel proud that Chinese and Orientals are doing great. But I think I am somebody unique, and I don't want people to think, "Oh my gosh, she is so conservative," or, "Her parents are really boring and conservative," because that's not true. People think I go home and study because I am darker and my hair is black. It doesn't mean I don't do the same things other teenagers do. People are not willing to open up and learn new things.

Tammi (Sumner, Washington): I think kids get prejudice from their parents. For example, Mexicans are stereotyped as lazy.

Angela (Battle Ground, Washington): My best friend is Jewish, and a lot of people say things that aren't nice. My parents are really prejudiced against her parents. My mom always makes comments like, "Can't Rachel do something about her nose?" People, even other minorities, don't realize that they are criticizing somebody else so blatantly.

Jennifer: I don't think anybody can honestly say, "I treat everybody equally."

San Francisco
Lowell High School

Gaby: It is not that the mothers don't want to have Oriental people in the PTA, but the Oriental parents themselves feel it is taboo. They don't seem to want to get involved. Even if you go to open house, most of the parents will be white. Maybe it is because of the language, but Orientals don't seem to want to participate as much as the Anglos.

Ann: I'm Oriental, and I have always been pushed into academics. Ever since I was 12, my dad would say, "Always take physics," or, "Study hard." That is why my brothers and sisters have always felt that their education is very important.

Dallas
A private home

How do minorities feel?

Homer Gifford (Cross-cultural specialist, Wycliffe Bible Translators): It's common for a minority group to think lowly of themselves. We were with a group of 100,000 Indians in southern Mexico. They had been conditioned for several hundred years to think their culture and language simply were not valid. They were very subservient.

Some groups have maintained their identity and are very

64

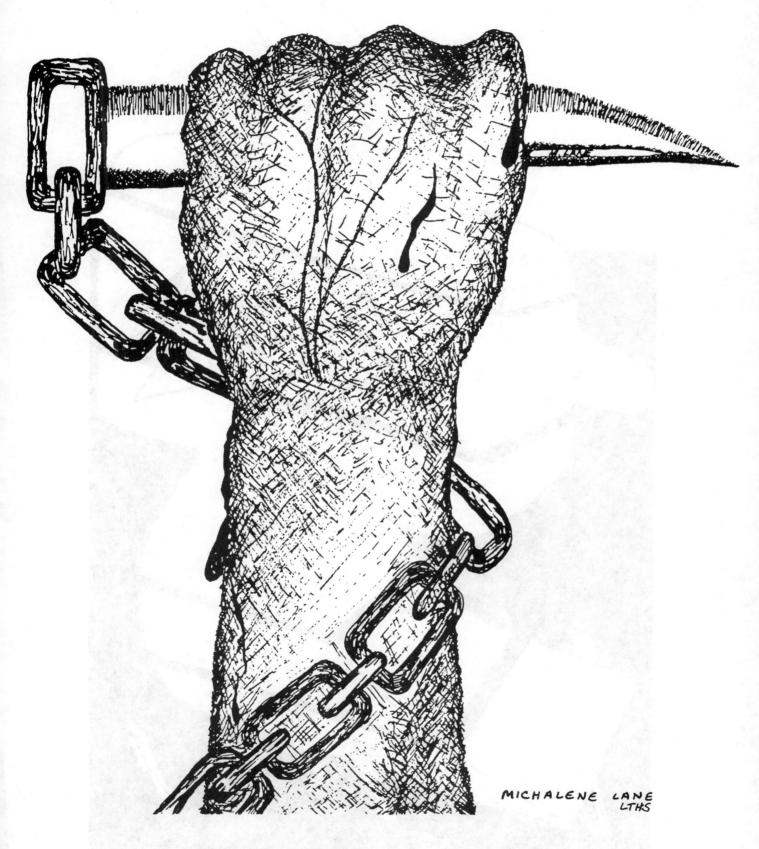

MICHALENE LANE
LTHS

Majorities and Minorities

proud....The Mixtecos,...for instance, won't even permit foreigners to stay overnight in some places.

How did you feel as a minority?

Gifford: They saw me as knowing everything and having everything. They came to me as a counselor, a minister, a mechanic, and a doctor. I filled those roles because no one else would attempt them. I didn't feel a part of that culture for a very long time. When I first came back to the States six years later, I felt totally out of touch here. I felt like an Indian in the middle of a foreign country. I felt very alone, very timid, very backward.

Do immigrants to the U.S. have the same feelings?

Gifford: Minority people tend to feel threatened and do not have a good sense of who they are. They tend to retreat to the people who know their language and have their culture. If they can develop enough confidence from that base to reach out, then they can integrate—become bi- or multi-cultural. But as long as they are in that threatened profile, they will tend to relate only when necessary to the outside world.

How can you encourage minorities to mix with other groups?

Gifford: In my intercultural relations class I tell them we're all equal. So far we don't feel that. Most people have a very Archie Bunker-ish attitude, whether they want to or not, and usually communicate their critical superior attitude more subtly than Archie. Their nonverbal communication, if not their words, reveals their aloofness and closed-mindedness.

Silver Spring, Maryland
Forcey Memorial Church

Glenda Jones (youth worker): Minorities should try to learn the language and to feel at home. But putting myself in their place, I'd want to keep my traditions.

Ron Jones (youth minister): They should try to fit in as much as possible without losing their individuality. It's a hard balance to achieve.

How much should minorities change their traditions?

Glenda: If they feel more comfortable in traditional dress, then that's fine.

Ron: If it's not a compromise to wear American dress, then it enhances their acceptability. It doesn't raise a red flag in others' minds that this person is different. People react to differences.

Glenda: We did a retreat for Korean people, and they did their prayers in Korean first and English next. I thought, "They're doing this for us." Then I found out that the children didn't know Korean. There has to be a balance.

Ron: They probably feel as American as we feel American, yet they still feel outside the American culture as far as total acceptability.

Jews

Portland, Oregon
A private home

Scott: Judaism is something that my parents tell me I am rather than something I feel. My mom thinks it's very important to go to the synagogue on the holidays. We go twice a year. She doesn't know what the holidays are about, and I don't either. But we have an obligation to go.

One of the things you have to do, being Jewish, is go to synagogue and listen to the boring sermon, even if you don't understand the words. It's just part of being Jewish. I'm pretty turned off by that part of it.

I wouldn't mind knowing more about Judaism, but it's not one of my priorities. It's just something I am, but it's not something I want to work at being. I don't pay much attention to it, but I don't hide it. I go to the services and do my duty as a Jewish person. Judaism plays the biggest part in my life around Hanukkah when you get presents.

Why do you feel you have to keep Jewish traditions?

Scott: Because of my parents and because I don't want to break with tradition. I don't think I'm ready to become an atheist. Probably when I'm on my own, I won't go to synagogue as much, if at all. I'll probably retain Jewish identity. In my heart, I see myself as Jewish even though I don't practice my religion or know about my religion as much as I should.

Judaism identifies me with a bunch of people, and I am not alone. If I need to, I can fall back to Judaism. I have pride in the past. I don't have pride in holidays which I don't understand.

How do Jews feel about the celebration of Christmas?

Scott: I don't think most Jewish people feel disoriented during Christmas because we have Hanukkah. I have a friend who gets really upset because he sees all the trees, ornaments, and hype about Christmas but doesn't see anything about Hanukkah. He doesn't think it's fair that people pay so much attention to the Christian religion, partially because he doesn't think the Christian religion has a right to be in existence.

He's told me that if he could go back right now in time, he'd go back and kill Jesus Christ. He's very anti-Christian. He doesn't think that there should be any religion other than Judaism. Also, he thinks that all other people are inferior. I think he is weird.

Both of us, though, would be insulted if someone tried to conform us to Christianity. It's like asking Americans if they want to become Russians. It's something you wouldn't even consider.

Would you ever marry a non-Jew?

Scott: Yes. I would think my parents wouldn't care—"It's nice if you marry a Jewish girl, but if you don't, that's okay." The only problem would be getting married. There's nobody to marry you except a judge. I've argued with my rabbi that I don't think it's fair. Intermarriage isn't accepted. Religion is not that big of a deal. It's something that you choose to be involved in. You should direct religion, not be directed by religion.

My friend's mother won't talk to her daughter because she married a non-Jew. He doesn't know where his sister is now.

Would you encourage your children to keep Jewish traditions?

Scott: Kids need direction. You can't just say, "Go out and find your way." You can tell them they're Jewish and show them Jewish culture. I don't think you can say, "You're Jewish. You have to be Jewish for the rest of your life."

I might take them to the synagogue and to the holidays. If they like what they see, they can do it. I'm not going to force them.

Minneapolis
Temple Isreal

Michael Gilbert (associate director of informal education): The survival of the American Jewish community is threatened. People are no longer identifying themselves as Jewish, and through intermarriage they are losing their Jewish identity.

My major goal, especially being an informal educator, is to make possible a teen Jewish identity. Rather than telling them they have to confine their likes to things that are Jewish, I tell them to make the things that are already in their lives Jewish. We need to make Judaism something kids can meet partway, rather than ask them to go all the way to something which is outside of their lives.

Judaism has something to say to them about issues that affect their lives—questions about sexuality, questions about substance abuse, and questions about how they relate to each other.

Does society misunderstand Jewish culture?

Gilbert: Misconceptions come up at particular times of the year, like at Christmas. I have a ninth-grader who came to me this year very confused. She was in choir, and it was time for the Christmas pageant. Her choir teacher, in an effort to be fair, asked the student to find a Hanukkah song to sing. I spoke to the choir teacher and said the student didn't think it was right. It set her apart. That makes our kids feel really out of place. There shouldn't be religious songs in the public schools, period.

I have a lot less trouble with the idea of singing something like "Jingle Bells," "White Christmas," or "Silver Bells" than something like "Little Drummer Boy" or "O Come All Ye Faithful." Again this is a separation of church and state question.

There's no time when Jewish kids feel stranger or more out of place than at Christmas. It makes our kids feel like foreigners. The U.S. is supposed to be a country in which there is no established religion, but this breaks down completely at Christmas.

At some time around age five or six, every Jewish kid goes through a crisis with his or her parents. The kid says, "Oh, I wish I were Christian because it looks like so much fun. Why can't we celebrate Christmas?" Hanukkah is a very minor holiday which has to be inflated because it competes with Christmas. It's not traditional to give gifts at Hanukkah. In the broad scheme of things, it is the least important of the Jewish holidays.

How important is education in Jewish culture?

Gilbert: It is definitely a part of our culture. While I'm proud of the extent to which Jewish tradition has always encouraged learning, it has its down side too.

Most of my kids have a high expectation of achievement that is a natural part of their environment. And I'm not sure that's good. Some of my most troubled kids go to the best school in town. Some of those kids feel the pressure to achieve.

What's the difference between being Jewish in the Midwest and being Jewish in New York City?

Gilbert: It's much easier growing up Jewish in New York because there are millions of Jewish people around. There's less of that feeling of being an outsider. It's incredible for me to walk around New York. There are so many synagogues. There are so many people speaking Hebrew. There are more than one or two places in town where you can get a kosher meal.

But most of the Jewish kids that I know who grew up in a really small town grew up with a really strong identification of being Jewish because it's been forced on them. We are a people who have survived on the basis of oppression. One of the dangers in America is that we are so readily accepted by the society that we are in danger of losing our own identity. That's why there is so much concern about encouraging Jewish kids to hang on to their Jewish identity.

Minneapolis
B'nai B'rith Anti-Defamation League of Minnesota and the Dakotas

Morton Ryweck (executive director): The main forms of discrimination today manifest themselves in vandalism, violence, and threats. Every year there are more than 1,000 incidents reported to us throughout the country. It could be a swastika put up on Jewish-owned buildings. I recently had a call that someone with a high-powered rifle shot at a Jewish school. Luckily it happened over the weekend, and no one was hurt.

The violent groups, fortunately, are pretty small in number. The Order killed a Jewish talk show host in Denver recently. As to why they've grown recently, part of it may be desperation that they're not gaining headway.

The subtle forms of prejudice are more difficult to deal with. We deal with that by educating people—through editorials, letters to the editor, and articles—as well as by working with schools and church groups.

We try to mobilize the community to understand that bigotry is beyond the pale of rational behavior. We try to bring minorities and majorities together also. Unfortunately, it's just not enough to lower the barriers. Positive programs are needed.

Muslims

Chicago suburb
A Muslim home

Mudassarah: Freshman and sophomore years, a lot of people called me Gandhi because the movie had just come out. And I'd come home yelling, "Mom, why do I have to keep wearing this scarf?"

Haroon: It gets bad sometimes because not just peers create prejudices, but sometimes the teachers think that the American culture is the best culture. They don't realize that other cultures can be different.

Iqbal: A lot of times in world history class, there'd be a tiny section on Islam in a huge book.

Haroon: I don't think prejudice is just racial. For example, during the Iranian hostage crisis, an Albanian Islamic center around here was torched to the ground.

Iqbal: When Haroon and I were in high school during the Iranian crisis, people would call us Iranian or they'd call us hostage-taker. And now with all the things that are going on with Kadhafi, it seems that people are almost finding things to perpetuate the misunderstanding of Islam and prejudice toward Muslims.

Haroon: A lot of them don't even know the difference between Muslim and Hindu. To them, it's all the same: "You're different."

Iqbal: To them, we're all cow-worshipers. It's very difficult to deal with prejudice.

Haroon: A lot of the confusion comes from the media, which perpetuates the idea of what Islam is. People in America have this view that all Muslim men have four wives who wait on their every need.

That's just not true. During the '84 elections, Mondale had to return two campaign contributions from Arab-Americans because of pressure from the press. It was an obvious racist gesture.

Naveed: If there is a Muslim military action, the media call them terrorists. But if there is an IRA action, they call them the Irish Republican Army.

Haroon: People don't understand Islam. They associate it with a religion. They don't realize that it's people. They don't realize that Islam is one of the world's largest religions. If Catholicism and Christianity are considered separate, then it is the world's largest. They don't realize that there's a common background behind Judaism, Christianity, and Islam.

How can Muslims overcome the misconceptions?

Arifa: The best thing is to point out the things you have in common with other people so you have something to share—so you can communicate. Then you can point out that there are differences.

Mudassarah: What most people think of you relates to what they see in the news. If they see something about Libya, they put a tag on you—"You're one of them." People often stare at me because I wear a scarf to school. They think, "Oh, so you're one of those." You really have to stick up for yourself. There are a lot of times when people would just pull the scarf off. I'd be so mad, and a couple of my friends would tell me to calm down. Then I would go to the person who did it and ask why. They usually don't have a reason.

What cultural conflicts do Muslims have?

Mudassarah: One big problem is trying to stay Muslim. Muslims here have lost their identity by adopting a lot of non-Islamic ways. They try to please their friends and act like them.

Haroon: Alcohol and dating are the two main things in high school. They're strictly forbidden in Islam. There's a lot of misunderstanding and prejudice. Since we can't socialize in the usual ways, we have to transcend these barriers and go into athletics or other activities to be accepted.

But a lot of kids who drink start putting pressure on you because they succumbed. Sometimes they invite you to go out and get drunk, and they can't understand why you don't want to.

Arifa: For women, there are a lot of dress restrictions, like covering your hair. You stick out. That causes a lot

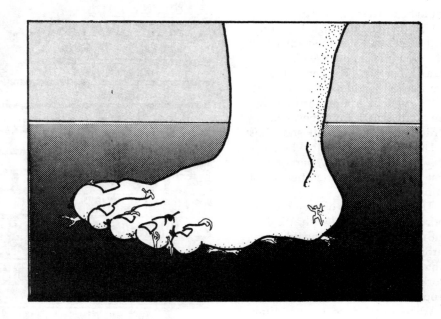

of problems because you may get ridiculed for what you do and what you believe. So people change the way they dress so they won't be made fun of at school.

Mudassarah: But if you really stick up for yourself, you'll have friends.

Iqbal: Sometimes the only way to transcend that kind of pressure is to try and elevate other aspects of getting along, like going to parties but not drinking or dating.

Haroon: But those are more superficial. If you make strong friendships, people will look beyond the restrictions and look at who you really are. And they'll respect you for it, maybe not at first, but eventually they will.

Iqbal: In high school, nobody ever asked me about Islam. Nobody ever asked me, "What's your religion about? Why can't you drink?" Now that I'm in college I've found it much easier to transcend the barriers, much easier to make friends. In college, they're much more concerned about your faith and beliefs.

It's important not only to have Christian friends but Muslim friends, too. It helps to be able to

talk to someone who knows what you're going through. A lot of the lighter Asians have an easier time fitting in. On the surface, they have more opportunity to fit in if they forsake their background and religion, but that creates an even greater pressure to conform.

Haroon: In high school, I often wondered why I was not dating, because there was so much pressure to date. But looking back, I realize that it's better that I didn't because marriage in Islam is prearranged.

In the Islamic center, it's taboo to talk to girls. It's okay to do it a bit, but people really get irritated if you do it a lot. But at school, it's okay. It didn't bother me. My parents probably didn't like it a lot.

Iqbal: I got into trouble for listening to different kinds of music. It's still unresolved whether rock is acceptable or not. A lot of people contend that it's the lyrics. Others contend that it's simply un-Islamic. I had a difficult time trying to deal with that. I think the Muslims of the new generation find music much more acceptable than our parents do. Dancing may be a different matter.

Haroon: A lot of the lyrics are contrary to Islamic views, but if you listen to the song and realize that lyrics are not guidance, then it's okay.

How do Muslims feel about those Muslims who have sacrificed their cultural identity?

Haroon: The ones I know I've lost respect for. They are not officially outcasts, but people tend to avoid them.

Arifa: Everyone else can survive, but they submit to pressure. It shows how weak their faith was. It's hard to associate with someone when your beliefs are totally different.

Haroon: It also makes the job twice as hard for us. They come up to us and say, "Hey, we're having a party, want something to drink?" You're trying to defend your beliefs, and someone who was one of your own tries to change you. You lose all respect for them.

Mudassarah: But they kind of have a tougher time because people come up to them and ask them, "How come you don't wear a scarf? Why don't you dress the way she does?"

Haroon: The ones who abandoned our religion totally used to come to the center, but now they're out going to parties. They're just dying to fit in, at all costs.

Arifa: And even if we don't shun them, they don't want to associate too much with us because people might think they still believe in the old customs.

What are the benefits of being Muslim in America?

Arifa: People here don't have a strong faith in God. It's just something in name. Religion helps you because you still have your faith in God even if you don't have a lot of friends. If you get in an argument with your friend about religion or beliefs, if your faith is strong enough, you won't change.

Iqbal: We have quite a bit of knowledge. We're not prejudiced against the East or the West. We have the best of both worlds.

Filipinos

Chicago
New Expression office

Glibel: When we first came here, we were the oddballs. I would feel different because my family was so un-Americanized. We're completely changed now, but not in our philosophies or principles. We still know that we have to go to college, but at the same time we are allowed to date. It's only the language and some of the everyday attitudes toward things that have changed.

But my sister still can't sleep over at anyone's house or share her clothes with her friends. My mother doesn't believe in that. She says, "I don't let you out because this is not the Philippines. You don't know how bad it is here." But a friend visited the Philippines last year and said the crime was very bad. I told my mom, but she didn't believe me.

How difficult is it to adjust to American culture?

Glibel: It was slow. When I was in eighth grade, I had long hair because in the Philippines, girls always have long hair. It was so weird because we didn't change from the time I was in fifth grade to the time I was in eighth grade. We were here for three years, and we still looked like we just got off the boat. Once I got into high school, I left my neighborhood and went downtown. I started seeing other people from other neighborhoods. That's what is so nice about magnet schools. With that, I changed drastically.

Because of me, my family changed, too. They're becoming Americanized so fast, so abruptly. I feel sorry for my mom because she never has had time to catch up. She's still trying to learn English.

What are the differences in education between the Philippines and the U.S.?

Glibel: I was in both public and private schools in the Philippines. The public schools were as strict as the private schools. They check your nails. They put a lot of emphasis on students' achieving. I always took it for granted that I'd go to college.

Kids here seem to have so many choices—"I'll go to college, but I want to travel first." I told my mom, "I need a year off to find myself." She said, "Glibel, you don't need yourself. You never had it anyway." She said I had to go to college.

The standards are much better over there. They have only six grades in elementary school. Here you have eight. Everything is more condensed, and you learn more. There is a lot of structure. Kids are afraid to break away from that structure. At the same time they want to because it is so strict. It's a third world country, and there is a lot of hunger. They see hunger, and they want to achieve something. They really listen to their parents if they want to do anything with their lives. Over here, it's different. You get a job that pays five dollars an hour. You can get by with that.

My friends wrote me from my boarding school. It's an all-girls school. They had a prom. They sent me a picture of girls dancing with girls. They couldn't take dates. It's not allowed.

Why is adjustment more difficult for the older generation?

Glibel: They are trying to cling to the better times. My mom was always saying that it's bad here and that it's better over there, but she's getting the hang of it. She's much more open about things. It's harder for the older generation because they have those half-remembered, half-made-up golden days. They cling to that like we cling to our teddy bears.

Asians

Maple Grove, Minnesota
A private home

Huynh Cong-Duc: In my country, everybody prayed to Buddha and prayed by Buddha's law. It was really hard for me to change my attitude when I came to America. When we came here, we didn't see any temples. We just saw churches. I was a Buddhist, but I'm a Christian now.

Phea Poch: I was a Buddhist, too. But as far as religion, it's not much of a difference. It was easy for me to change. Christianity and Buddhism both allow you to live the good way and make a good living.

In Asia, young unmarried girls and boys seldom talk in public. Here people talk, kiss, or do more. Sometimes it's shocking. But if something fits me, I stay along with it. If it doesn't, I go. That's how I get along.

Gail Lando (teacher): I have a different viewpoint. I'm both Asian and American, but mostly American. When Asians come into our country, they're a little shy. They're a little more private than Americans. Our styles are different.

Phea: In Asia, normally the man cannot even touch the woman. If the parents see it, the man would be in trouble. Men have to be gentle and humble.

Huynh: If you're over 20, you can do whatever you want. But if you're under 19, get married first then have a kid after. If you have a kid first, get out of the house. The man has responsibility for that child.

How much pressure is there to conform to American society?

Huynh: I still keep my culture. When I go out, I don't do anything in public.

Sangraphim Lah-Phosa: This country is freedom. That's why I came. I live for my culture, for myself.

Huynh: Most of the freedoms are for the people who have money. Money can't buy freedom, but some of your freedoms come easier if you have money. You don't have to worry about food. When you go shopping, you can buy anything. Money can help you get out of your country. It can buy you a plane ticket.

Lando: I used to give a writing assignment asking people to write about an experience in which they learned something. My American students wrote about baseball games and vacations, but an Asian student wrote about the time he crossed the Mai-Cong River and his mother was killed and he couldn't stop to mourn or bury her. I read about women who were raped and people who left everything behind because America was a free country. They did it all for freedom.

What problems does the language barrier cause?

Phea: When I first came here, I didn't know much English. Even what I knew, I couldn't understand. I couldn't talk much. Sometimes it's so hard to understand, even when I study harder and harder.

Lando: I see it a lot, too. I'm working with a Vietnamese woman who has five kids. Her English is about Level I. When her eight-year-old boy comes home from school and she tries to talk to him in Vietnamese, he says, "Momma, I can't understand you." Even when she talks in English, he can't understand her.

As we work together, we have developed ideas about how to handle other problems.

On teaching English

Lando: We owe a tremendous debt to the kids of the world. And there is money to teach kids English. Our country has created races of refugees. The amount spent on the war in Vietnam was huge. If we could spend fortunes on killing

people, we could easily spend fortunes on redeeming those people whose lives have been shattered by our actions. If every American has to make a sacrifice so we can teach Asian kids English, so be it.

On handling prejudice

Phea: When someone comes up to me and says, "I don't like you—you're Asian," at first I might feel upset. Then I'd think maybe he's not in such a good mood or maybe he's having some troubles at home.

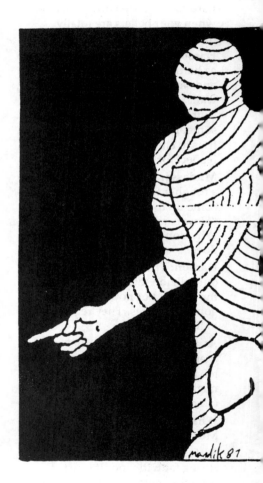

That way I avoid judging people—
it's how I get along.

On sharing culture
Sangraphim: When I came here, I
wanted to offer everything I could to
get along and to help make this
country the best in the world. If you
want to know about my language,
I'll teach you. If you want to know
about spicy food, I'll teach you. You
must ask.

Compiled by Dave Seng

Chapter 5.

Individuals and Gangs

Cool Z is The Man on 163rd Street. He's small and skinny, but he's got a razor scar on his forehead that looks like a frown, and he's got a new Buick. Z runs the rockhouse on our block. He sells the coke rocks right out the front door and runs the neighborhood like it's his personal kingdom.

Cool Z shot my friend Ronny right between the eyes. I was there. I saw it. There was no blood or nothing, just a round, black hole over Ronny's nose. After Ronny fell on the floor all crumpled up, Cool Z put the gun down on the table and smiled at me. He pointed at Ronny, then whirled his finger by his head, like he was saying Ronny was crazy.

Ronny wasn't crazy. He was just real stupid because he thought he could rip off Cool Z. See, Ronny worked for the South Commandos, Z's "organization," like he called it. In the house they have maybe 15 guys, scoring the rocks, handling the money, keeping watch on the street. Everybody has guns, mostly .45's and Uzi's. Guns and a lot of money.

More money than we have. My mama hasn't worked in three years. If we didn't get food stamps, we wouldn't eat. She says I got to educate myself and get out of here, and I'm trying, but these dudes run around like rich white men in their slick threads and Cadillacs. It makes you think.

Ronny was making $6,000 a week. At least that's what he told me. I believed him. He went out three weeks ago and bought a gold Fleetwood with wire wheels and a padded roof—$30,000 paid in cash. His brother had to buy it for him 'cuz you need a driver's license, and Ronny was only 15.

That's the car I took when I cut out after Cool Z shot Ronny. He asked me where the shit was, and I got real nervous and said I thought Damon, that's Ronny's brother, had it. Cool Z smiled again and said, "Okay." That's all he said—"Okay."

So Cool Z didn't check the Fleetwood and find the $200,000 worth of rock in the trunk. I left fast.

Ronny had been hiding the stuff a little at a time over the last few months. He was going to sell it to some dude up north. We were going to go this weekend.

He always told me this stuff 'cuz I'm not really a South Commando. I sort of hang out. I do some favors for Z—wash his car, run some errands. I was around so much I guess most of them thought I was a member. I do claim them for backup, though, like when I went to visit my aunt in Bell Gardens and some guys were going to butt me. I said Commandos, and they backed right off. My mama don't want me in a gang, and I'm not, really. But it's easier for all of us this way, with me sort of in.

At least I've always been taught that it would make my life easier. You don't end up getting smashed against a wall like Marvin. He was always working on some deal, taking care of Number One, he said. He was real stuck-up, said he didn't need no gang. They smashed him with a car up against a brick wall, broke his back.

And you don't get scared away like my sister. She was living with one of the Commandos, and he used to beat her up pretty bad. When she said she was leaving, he said he'd kill her. She knew he wasn't playing so she had to go live up in Oakland, and she still thinks he might get her.

I didn't think I should go home after I left the rockhouse. I had to find some place to hide so I broke into school 'cuz it's summer and no one's around. I have to chill for a while and think what to do. I got the coke with me in a plastic bag. I'm no dummy. I won't throw $200,000 down the toilet. I have an address for the dude up north. I left the wheels down by the loading dock.

I know Z's going to talk to Damon, probably kill him. He'll figure out where the rock is. I just hope he isn't going to mess with my mama or my little brother. I keep thinking about the way he smiled after he killed Ronny.

Last year I had class in this room at the end of the hall. It was Mr. Roland's class. In the morning we could hear his patent leather shoes clicking down the hallway. I hear footsteps like that right now. I know it's Cool Z. He's come to get the rock. But I keep hoping it's just the janitor.

Eric Kammerer

National Reactions—Conflicts

My friend Angelicko was a 15-year-old negro who lived in Chicago. Angelicko was never "into" gangs until he found himself with nothing else to do. . . .

Soon after that Angelicko was "hanging out" with a gang. Then soon after that, he "became" one of them. . . . Angelicko was so bored that he couldn't find anything else to do than become a "gang" member. . .and then get killed.

*Lalynn Bothwell, 15
Portage, Indiana*

Gangs are a threat to the community. They are usually low-class individuals with long greasy hair and dirty clothing. Gangs deal with drugs and even take it themselves. Some even carry the disease AIDS.

A very important part of their tasks involves stealing from ladies' purses and automobiles. They cause windows to break by using stones or bats.

Gangs in high schools are basically the same as the ones on the street. . . . They vandalize rooms and threaten to

beat upon others.

*17-year-old male
Pennsylvania*

I don't belong to a stereotypical street gang. I'm a punk. . . .Whenever you see someone with spiked hair. . .you feel that you can go up to him or her and say, "How's it going?" because that person believes, acts, and enjoys much of the same things I do. In a gang, you always have someone to call on if you

I USED TO LOOK UP TO MY OLDER BROTHER BECAUSE HE WAS IN A GANG...

NOW I LOOK DOWN ON HIM...

RIP (DEAD)

need help or you need to talk....

There are also a lot of complications. Once in Chicago, some friends of mine and I were walking around and saw two rival groups of skins (neo-Nazi punks who have shaved heads) start to go at it—canes flying, heads being bashed into brick walls, and a lot of blood. Then one of them recognized us and asked us to help him. We had to, or he'd get some friends and kick our asses good.... The violence from one rival gang to another is completely stupid. It's...a way to escape from your problems by giving someone else a problem.

Another problem is gang graffiti. Most of it is pretty mindless....I've done a lot of graffiti, but it's been political—statements on a fence like, "no war, no KKK, no fascist U.S.A."

Sandy Greenberg, 17
West Chicago, Illinois

You claim a barrio, or you're nothing. There are a lot of conflicts you have to go through with the other barrios, with the other low rider clubs, and surrounding towns....We...are the only organized hood. All the other patches thought that they could be Numero Uno. But they carried it to far extremes. They would crash parties just to cap off someone for the hell of it.

19-year-old male
Arizona

I moved into some new place....My new friends...asked me to join this gang, and I didn't want to turn them down....The people in it were very tough. They said, "If you're ever in some trouble, call on us to help you out."

I felt more protected. I felt more popular. Everyone knew me now. They wouldn't mess with me....

I was doing wrong, but it was fun. It made me laugh. Sometimes, I didn't want to do some of these things, but I did it to please my friends. It is really just all fun....

I've been in a detention center for a while. I've been to court.

17-year-old male
Indiana

Teenagers want to join "gangs" to become part of a group or to worship something....Gangs worship a leader just as many people worship God or Satanists worship Satan....

Many teenagers join gangs for protection or friends....They learn how to get along as part of a group.

Tina Blachly, 16
Portage, Indiana

Gangs...are all the same, wherever you go. I have many friends involved in ...a gang. They are all very nice people and have a very sensitive side to them.

Some of the guys in the gang...told me that they...weren't out to prove anything to anyone. They all hung around each other to keep each other company and party....

I've met other gang members who would kill someone if he wore the wrong colors in the wrong neighborhood.

I recently found out that in order to be a girl member of this gang, the girl must...have sex with each member of that gang....

Guys who are in a gang are usually the type who think they won't go anywhere in life. They all hang around each other for security. In reality that's the only time they talk big.

Alone, they're as scared as mice next to an elephant.

Carol Juarez, 16
West Chicago, Illinois

Women are raped almost on a daily basis by gangs. Buildings are destroyed; cars are stolen; and people are mugged.

Aaron Jarvis, 16
Portage, Indiana

To become a gang member, most people

KRISTIN WAIDE
LTHS

78

have to go through initiations. . . . I've never had any experience in being in a gang, but I tried to get into one. . . . For my initiation, they wanted me to break into a house, but I didn't do it. I didn't think it was worth a chance of getting in trouble with the police just to get into an immature gang.

> 16-year-old male
> Rhode Island

I know a guy whose father is into drugs, and he was put in jail recently. The father is hardly at home, and when he is, he doesn't pay much attention to his children. . . .

His son doesn't care if he gets himself into trouble. He belongs to a gang. . . . He just wants somewhere to go and something to do. There are many occasions when this guy gets into trouble, but to him, it's just his way of life. It is the way he grew up.

> Marci Villanueva, 16
> Portage, Indiana

Gangs let teenagers feel like they belong to a group. . . . A lot of gangs act really tough . . . but really they are the ones hurting inside.

> Brooke Agent, 17
> Sand Springs, Oklahoma

When I see the damage and trouble the Latin Kings have caused, I get very angry. Why must they destroy the property that my parents pay for? Every week it seems that this gang has painted some more graffiti or broken another window, yet the school does nothing to inhibit their actions.

Another problem the gang causes is racial unrest. Since almost all of its members are Hispanic, they feel that the school officials and Caucasian students are singling them out for harassment. I feel that this is not true.

> 17-year-old male
> Illinois

Gangs are a group of people that stick together as friends. This group also has trust for each other. When people think

of a gang, they think of people in leather jackets with chains and guns, but there are all kinds of gangs (groups). Some of the different groups are the jocks, the stuck-up people, and the brains.

The complications that these groups can face are that people in their gang (group) are the only people they talk to, and therefore, they leave the rest of the people in the world isolated.

> Dean Colavecchio, 18
> Cranston, Rhode Island

For some joining gangs is like a cry for help. They see no way to get the attention they crave so they act violently.

> Sherry Martins, 18
> West Chicago, Illinois

At my school, I see a lot of my white friends in gangs as well as Mexicans. . . . Most of their parents are divorced and have large families that don't pay any attention to them. . . .

> Sheryl Wilmer, 18
> West Chicago, Illinois

Discussion

Male, ex-gang member (Los Angeles): I ain't a gang banger anymore. I'm in a halfway house, putting in time for gang violence. I went up to the schoolhouse one day and started a riot, some power moves. They gave me four years for it. That's why I'm coming here.

Female (Oakland, California): My aunt just died. She was walking to the grocery store, and these guys were fighting over some girls. Some guys drove by in a black car and just started shooting. The second bullet hit my aunt. She didn't have anything to do with the guys. She just happened to be at the wrong place at the wrong time.

Male (Oakland, California): There was a big uproar at Rainbow Center.

I was on their turf. They started with sticks. One had a gun in his trunk, and I was right across the street from his car. He went to get it, but I ran to hide. When he started chasing me, I took some back cuts to my house. When I went back down again, there were a lot of police and an ambulance. That was almost my life right there. I don't go down there anymore.

Violence

Oakland, California
Fremont High School

Tanya: There've been so many shootings lately it's not funny. Five of my friends died over Christmas vacation. I never expected it.

Lisa: The last time I left New York, I was not involved with a gang. Some gang members chased some of my friends who grind base rocks. They broke out with guns, shot each other up, and three people I knew died. It was the last thing that happened to me before I left. Living around there, even if you don't grind or scramble for them, you get involved one way or another.

Kim: Yeah. One time at a fair, this little guy, I guess he was a Cousin, came over to a guy who goes to school here. All of a sudden they started fighting, and crowds of people went running and screaming. A man got cut with a bottle.

Tanya: Nobody at the fair was involved with the gang, but they were around at the wrong time and suffered.

Kim: Nine times out of ten in fights, none of the immediate gang members are hurt. It's the people around.

Tanya: Like she said, if you're in the area, or if you're their friend, you might as well say you're involved. One of my friends, who died on December 31, was by his friend's car with two of his buddies. They were just talking, and somebody going by shot up the car and shot the three of them.

Phil R.: Some of my close friends have died. The first time it was a shock, but after a while I realized that if they're going to get involved with gangs, this is going to be the consequence. It didn't really faze me.

Lisa: It always fazes me, especially if you see the people and the next thing they're dead. I hear it and see it all the time. I used to live in the middle of it, but it still kind of chips me out. These people are just so young, people I went to school with.

Phil B.: Yeah. It's a shock, we have to admit. We also have to admit that in a way we have become a little callous about all the killings. It's almost expected to happen. You're just waiting for it.

Tanya: You always know it's coming, but you don't expect it to be someone in your family or around the corner or down the street.

Lisa: The gangs in New York are more businesslike. In New York, if they killed someone, they did it for a reason. Out here they shoot because they like to shoot, and people get knocked off for no reason. In New York they run their gangs like a corporation. I lived in Sacramento, too. Out there they had some gangs, but they were pretty weak.

Los Angeles
World Christian Training Center in Watts

Quentin: Violence is how gangs talk to each other. Like, you write your gang name on the wall, and some other gang comes and writes theirs over it. It's called crossing out. The crossed-out gang goes out and attacks the other one.

Chris: Another source of conflict is, say, my club, the Westside Boys, goes to a party in East Los Angeles.

The Eastsiders don't like us because we're always taking over parties. When we show up, they start getting hostile and attacking. And half the time it's about drugs. You go over to my neighborhood, and they got gang members out there trying to hook you on. They got other people who'll cut you up. They start punching and fighting over drugs.

Chicago

Male mugging victim: I was coming home on the bus, and there's a stop after I get on where a lot of gang members get on. I was sitting toward the middle of the bus, and it wasn't really crowded. When we got to the stop, a lot of them got on. The bus driver is usually so scared when they get on that he just opens all the doors and doesn't make them pay.

They get on like a bunch of wild animals and rampage the bus. Whenever they see something they want, like an old lady with a purse, they just take the purse. Nobody can do anything because there are so many of them that they can get away with anything.

I was just sitting on the bus. I wasn't doing anything. It was cold then so I was wearing my coat, which has a lot of pockets on the chest. A lot of them started going into my pockets seeing what I had in there, but they were empty. My money was in my wallet in my pants pocket. They started asking me for money. I told them I didn't have any, but they didn't believe me so a lot of others started going through my pockets.

I was thinking, "Oh shit, what are they going to do now?" So I turned around and looked at them. There were so many of them that I was surrounded. I was the only white person on the bus. I got panicky. I didn't know what to do. All of a sudden I felt a punch on the

back of my head. I turned around to punch the guy back, but I couldn't tell who did it because there were so many of them.

Then all of them started punching me everywhere. I was trying to punch them back as best I could. Then I was on the floor, and they were stepping on me.

I was all black-and-blue for a while. I had to go to the hospital to get 20 X rays of my head because that's where they hit me. I looked like Rocky. My whole face was black-and-blue.

Now I'm more careful when I ride the bus. I sit at the front whereas before I used to sit toward the middle or toward the back. Now I've started recognizing which ones are the thieves. They have a method of pickpocketing: They drape their jackets over their hands and go into people's purses. Most of the old people don't realize until they're off the bus. Usually the other gang members cheer them on.

The bus driver didn't do anything when I got mugged. He has a button on his phone, which he can use for emergencies. He didn't use it. I was really pissed off. I reported him. There are a lot of robberies—pickpocketing and stuff—but what happened to me I don't see too often.

It would be really hard to improve security. It's just the way that those people were brought up. They think it's okay to do that. It's just their morals. Now there are police officers standing at bus stops. But there are only one or two police—no big deal. Nothing happens.

I want to get out of my neighborhood. We've been thinking about moving for a long time. We're going to move soon. I'm looking forward to it.

Attraction
Los Angeles

Terry: I started gang-banging because my big brother was a gang banger. He had a reputation. Everybody used to call him Big Booker and me Little Booker. They were always asking me, "Where's your bigger brother?" I wanted attention like he got so I started gang-banging. When I was gang-banging like him, people were getting killed. It was tough walking down the street because I might get shot up.

Wilmington, Delaware
State Department of Juvenile Services
John Henderson (director of a youth diagnostic center): Joining gangs could have something to do with lack of goals. There's an entire summer, and teens have nothing to do. Maybe they've gotten particular responses from the adult world, and that tends to coalesce them. Maybe the chicks think the guys in the gang are pretty neat, and then more guys join. So it's taking on a positive appearance to outsiders.

Fred Barnes (probation counselor): When you get a lot of people together like that, they try to relate past experiences. And once one adventure is over, they look for another one. When I was growing up, there were a series of groups, I guess you could call them gangs. They used to call themselves "The Dorm," which represents the place where they were living. They even had jackets with their name on it. If they saw someone with "The Dorm" on their jacket, they were all right. If not, they were outsiders.

I also know of several cases where kids went into other areas and got jumped. They'd come back, get their brothers and friends, and they'd have a gang. And they'd go out and get revenge. Then they'd kind of stay together. If anything like this ever happened again, they'd know the guys they could get together.

Oakland, California
Lisa: I think the attraction is the power. Most of the kids who are in gangs do come from poor backgrounds, and selling drugs is good money-making. You have a lot of authority. Nobody is going to bother you. It actually is kind of attractive. Everybody knows who you are walking down the street. "Don't mess with me."

It's not like you can't understand why—it's logical in a way. A lot of them, they don't have a chance to do anything else. They didn't go to school. I'm not going to excuse them for not going to school or not graduating. If they do graduate, it's with a D minus average. And this way they're making money. They've got girls, and the girls always want protection.

Tanya: My grandmother used to live in 69th Village so we all grew up together. Everybody in 69th Village formed a gang, and most people were expected to be in it. If you hang around at all, though you may not say you're with the gang, those on the outside may look at you and say you are. That happened with me. My father found out, and everything went haywire. The only reason I knew them was I grew up with them in the same area.

Lisa: When we stayed in Harlem, we had to move because of my cousin. He could have joined the gang if he wanted to even though we hadn't grown up in the neighborhood. We moved to that area, and all of a sudden, since he was a new guy in the area, he was prime picking. He was 15. It was

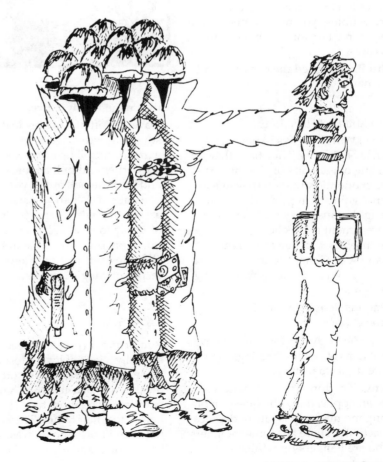

KEVIN JOHNSON
LTHS

Individuals and Gangs   *81*

time for him to join, and we had a lot of trouble that way. But, generally speaking, if you grow up with them, you are expected to join the gang.

Phil B.: If you don't, you are a traitor. I know a lot of people who are not directly in a gang, but they still claim them as backup in case something should happen.

Lisa: That causes problems, too. People don't like to be claimed if they're not in it.

Tanya: I know a mother of a gang member who is behind her son 100 percent. He can buy her $600 dresses. She knows where the money is coming from, but it's supplying things in the house so she doesn't care. If your parents are behind you, you go all the way. There's no one to stop you.

Lisa: Another reason for joining gangs is a lot of times you can't sell drugs unless you're a member: "You sell on my territory, I'll blow your ass away."

Phil B.: You need the backup. And the name.

Lombard, Illinois
Glenbard East High School

Dave: With the guys I know, it's a sense of identity. They have this feeling of general hopelessness that the economic situation they live in is not going to improve. They join gangs because they can't fight the government and police by themselves. Or they can't fight Gang A or Gang B across the street so they join one side to avoid being beaten up.

Magnus Seng (parent): For protection?

Dave: Yeah. And a lot of them have problems at home—beatings by parents, sexual abuse.

Seng: You don't "join." You don't file an application. The question of gang membership is one of degrees of activity. There are some members who are hangers-on, affiliates, but

they're not really active.

Dave: It's often a life-or-death situation. Either you represent their gang, or they'll take you down to the corner and pull a knife or a gun and beat the hell out of you until you submit. When you start associating with them, you're officially in a gang. I know a gang down on 47th Street, Satan's Disciples, who actually kept a record of gang members.

Los Angeles

Ron Brunner (project director): It's basically a lack of love. Most of these big guys I get in my office break down because they have a poor family relationship. They have hatred for their father. They might not even know who he was. They break down and cry right in this

office because they're nothing more than a scared little boy in a 6-foot, 200-pound frame.

Escape

Oakland, California

Lisa: It's almost a basic impossibility to just decide to get out. It can be done, though. If you're real deep in the gang and know all the business, you get beat up a few times. Then they might leave you alone. You might get killed. I've seen a lot of people who used to be in gangs, and now they just walk around the streets blitzed. The only people who get out of gangs grow out of them.

Tanya: A lot of times your parents say, "Get up. Let's go." The only decision you make is how to choose new friends and change your life. The only thing you can really do is go to a different community college or join the army.

Womazetta: My uncle was in a gang when he was younger, and he got out. Now he's a doctor. He just doesn't associate with them anymore.

Dave: If you're in a Chicago gang and you move out to the suburbs, they won't bother you. But if you go back to the city, you're still part of the gang. You could be wearing a $500 suit, but you'd better be prepared to associate with the gang.

Seng: A lot of people may be ready to leave the gang, but they don't have any alternatives—no job, no home, nothing.

Los Angeles

Terry: It used to be hard. They could ask you to take out somebody you know. If you don't do it, you could get killed.

Sergio: Like he said, back then it was hard. In my neighborhood, once you're in, you're always in. If you wanted to get out, you'd be either dead or half dead. That's in my neighborhood. If you were a Westsider, we look at the situation and say, "He's moving into another neighborhood. You know if he's going to need help, he's going to call us."

But you're a Westsider, regardless. In that gang, if you want out, you end up dead. They pump you, spit on your face. They'll pretend they don't know you. They won't count you out, but they won't count you in. "You want to be a Westsider, join in. If you want out, then every time we see you, we're going to spit on your face, call you a punk, and hurt your friends and family."

Wilmington, Delaware

Tim Brandau (treatment superintendent): I think that most of the people who go through our system grow up to be productive adults.

Barnes: It could be counseling, or it could be that they're just growing out of it. I think that's another misconception people often have—that juvenile delinquents grow up to be criminals. They might continue into their early adult years, but by their late twenties, they're tired of running, breaking in, and getting in trouble with the law.

Identity

Lombard, Illinois

Womazetta: I go to the city every weekend. When I walk around my grandmother's neighborhood, I see gang members all wearing red jackets and red bandannas. Another gang wears different things.

Brad: You can't really identify them by clothes.

Dave: Most definitely you can identify them by clothes. Most hard-core gang members represent their gangs outwardly. But there are a lot of associate gang members who participate in some of the crime—not the killings, but some of the robberies. They won't come out with a tattoo or the colors, but they'll associate with gangs. The real hard-core gang members will dress in their colors in their neighborhood usually—not when they're out. People have the idea that 40 guys stand on street corners. That never happens.

Wilmington, Delaware

Susan Greenstern (executive assistant): There is a lot of controversy around here about what a gang is. How do you define a gang? Your sociological definition

is one thing, the way the press views groups of people in Wilmington is another. A group of people—is that a gang?

Brandau: They give themselves a name, too.

Barnes: In the New Castle area, there's always one guy on top. He's usually gifted socially. He can speak well. Guys can look up to him, whether they're older or younger. They can look up to and respect him. The kids who grew up in a part of New Castle called Rose Hill don't want to have kids from Wilmington on their turf. That seems to be a lot of what it's about. There's a number of kids who aren't into it, but they just live in the area.

Los Angeles

Christopher (ex-gang member): A gang is a group of individuals with talent and an overabundance of energy that needs to be channeled. In my neighborhood we created our own gang with our block and the next couple of blocks. Our members didn't come from poor families only. Some were middle-class. Their parents had to go to work, and they didn't have anything to do but run the streets at night.

New York City
Youth Action Program in Harlem

Johnny Rivera (youth counseling coordinator): Gangs tend to be violent and tend to have antisocial behavior. Friendship groups come together and do not necessarily intend to terrify people, beat up on other people, or take money. But they probably involve themselves in getting high. Some gangs have a definition of what are now called colors: a jacket with a symbol and their name on their back. Friendship groups are people who get to know each other and get together as friends.

My only concern is that if we see

a group of young people on the street around the neighborhood here, they will be stereotyped as violent young people. And I say that a gang can organize and renovate a building. There is a clear example here in the community of a gang that did that. The gang might have criminal records. A gang might have recognition as a group while a friendship group may not.

Orlando Santiago (program director): I would differ with Johnny's opinion of a gang and a friendship group. I don't think they are different at all. The word "gang" is just a way society says that this group of people is other than the norm. I think that groups can be viewed as friendship groups and gangs. These groups of people are looking for identities and have been able to find them within that group. If the perception of the people who are approaching this group is negative, there is more tendency to call them a gang. What we try to do here at Youth Action Program is remove that idea. They are friendship groups. They are approachable.

Atlanta

Theresa Price (investigator): A lot of them join in what we call social groups. They wear identifying jackets and get involved in shoplifting and rumbles. In reality, all they are is a street gang.

Future

Oakland, California

Tanya: Gangs are wearing thin to me. Back in the seventies I understand there were a lot. But there are more now. And they've just been growing and growing.

Phil B.: From what I understand, as far as the black community goes, there wasn't that much. I'm not sure, but all the Mexicans were pretty much united. As the Mexican population started growing, they started claiming Eastside Oakland. After that they started dividing into streets—36th, 38th, 41st, 65th, 96th. They used to be pretty mean, too.

Lisa: That's why I think some of them are going to get power and lose power, but I think there will basically always be some gangs around. Like 20 years from now, Sixty-nine will not be the reigning gang around here, but there will be one around.

Tanya: Will they continue to grow, get bigger and bigger as time goes on? I don't think so.

Lisa: There'll always be gangs. Different things for different times. Next we'll have terrorism.

Kim: They're coming up with all these ways to stop the gang members from having gangs and everything. I think they want people who are independent. They want to have all these hit men. They have them now, but it's not independent business. That's what it's going to be. Like *Scarface*.

Lombard, Illinois

Womazetta: In the city, gangs are not as bad as they used to be. My mom used to tell me stories about the gangs when she was growing up. You couldn't even call what we have today gangs.

Dave: From what I know of gang lore, back in the late sixties and early seventies there were larger groups, two or three thousand people, in one gang. Today, it's diversified. There is still a lot of street fighting, but they're past sticks and stones and up to guns, knives, and drug dealing. They're no longer beating each other up to control a block. It's to get control of narcotics.

Los Angeles

Christopher: Statistics say that by the year 2000, Los Angeles is going to have more people than New York. I've been to New York. If there's going to be a change in the next decade, it's going to be one hell of a situation here.

Suburbia

Lombard, Illinois

Brad: About the gangs out here, from the people I know in them, they're not gangs so much as people hanging around, pretending to rebel, and trying to gain acceptance.

Dave: It's an identification, especially in this suburb. In suburbs closer to the city, they're legitimate gangs. As for the gangs out here, I have a big fear that in a few years there will be some legitimate, hard-core gangs.

Seng: You've got some already.

Brad: Right now it's just groups of people getting together.

Dave: No, you have a lot of gangs out here, but they're not outward.

Seng: The question is really whether the gang moves out here or whether the gang gets going from kids who are already situated out here. You have some phenomenon where gangs are moving from one

neighborhood to another but not to any great extent. The needs of suburban kids are the same as those of urban kids—a sense of belonging, of purposefulness, of meaning.

Dave: Suburban gangs around here come out and sit by the Du Page Theater. My friend JJ, he's a Disciple, just laughs about them. He went up to a couple of guys on the corner by the theater and gave them the Disciples handshake and they didn't even know it. He was insulted because they were impersonating his gang. It's like they were insulting his family. The Disciples are a really big gang.

The Lombard gangs that are using their symbols and impersonating them don't realize the magnitude of their mistake. JJ could have gone back and gotten his friends, who all have cars and guns.

Seng: It's considered an insult. The graffiti and handshake are part of the gang identity. When that is insulted, members take it personally.

Womazetta: My grandmother lives on the south side so I've seen enough gang symbols to know what they're like. The ones out here are a joke.

Solutions
Oakland, California

Tanya: You can spread the word—"Don't get involved"—among friends, neighbors, and family. I tell my brothers. Another good solution would be to make a law where if you're under 18 and have a certain number of counts against you, you get shipped to the Army. They could make themselves useful. They already know how to use guns well enough, and they would make money.

New York City

Santiago: Teens aren't given enough credit for what they can do. They have no say in decisions at home because parents feel they're incapable. The Youth Action Program is unique because it reverses that. It allows young people to get around and make decisions.

Rivera: We approach groups of young people on the street, develop rapport with them, and ask them how they would like to see the community improved. They came up with the idea of renovating some old buildings so people could live in them. Prior to YAP, I don't think there have been too many groups employing teens in the whole process: thinking about building, taking the steps, and seeing it through.

Orlando: A successful community improvement project is something that is incredible for young people. Last year we organized a group of young people into a coalition. The purpose was to get a group of young people together to petition the city government to include $10 million in the budget for youth employment, specifically house rehabilitation. We held candlelight vigils at City Hall when they were going through budget hearings. When the budget was passed, there was $4 million for youth employment. This year we got $12.3 million included in the budget.

I think that those kinds of successes are important. It shows that we can empower our young people, who are going to be our future leaders, to take directions that are positive.

Los Angeles

Terry: Young guys who are coming up are going through the same thing I was, but they won't listen. They want to experience everything for themselves. But we can try to talk to them.

Sergio: We have to give them a role model, somebody to look up to. Somebody that's not into drugs or gang-banging.

Christopher: We need role models

in the minority community other than just in sports because everybody can't get into sports. We need role models in the medical field and other knowledge fields.

Los Angeles

Brunner: I'm a three-time loser myself, an ex-con. The last time was for attempted murder. It was at the time of sentencing that I asked the Lord to come into my life. The bottom line was I had to spend 15 years of my life in the state pen, but I got saved.

Compiled by Dave Seng

Solutions

I think that society should make a place for gangs to hang out and meet. If they had a place to meet, they could probably work out their differences without fighting. They could just have arm wrestling or play a game. . . .

They could have a place inside this building for all of the gangs to write their graffiti on. . . . They could paint the outside the same way. That gives the gangs a creative way to get rid of their aggression.

Sean Minerd, 18
Uniontown, Pennsylvania

Everyone wants to "fit in," and gangs might accept people others wouldn't. When I feel that I don't "fit in," I feel like my whole world is caving in on me, and there is no escape.

For some kids, a gang is the only place they can turn to for what they would call "love."

Julie Foster, 16
Portage, Indiana

The gang members here are pretty cool—not too many fights. You have the Low Riders for instance. All they care about is their pride and joy. . .their low rider. One car club would go against another to see who or what club can hop the highest. There may be some fights but none too serious.

Charley James Hines, 17
Tucson, Arizona

The law should somehow or someway break these threatening groups up. For example—prison terms up to at least 20 years.

Becky Brangard, 17
Fairchance, Pennsylvania

Many who join gangs today. . .have a chip on their shoulder, which brews inside of them until they no longer have control over their senses. They decide to get revenge. Others just want to pass the time. . . .

Adults today are more concerned with telling a kid what he has done wrong, than. . .with taking steps to prevent what he has done from happening again.

Mike Terwilliger, 15
Portage, Indiana

Gangs help people in the streets to feel like they belong in the real world. . . . You feel needed and wanted. . .instead of being pushed around.

Dorris Ho, 18
Carol Stream, Illinois

I was once in a "gang," but this was a weight-lifting organization. Instead of fighting, we would challenge other gangs at the gym.

Mike Hudgins, 16
Portage, Indiana

I think gangs are becoming extinct, if they aren't already. If there are any gangs today, they should not be tolerated. They only cause worry and pain. . . .

Gangs were popular in the 60s and 70s, but people are changing their ways in the 80s. . . . Society is more educated today than it was 20 years ago, and therefore, people do not form gangs.

Gangs were a form of insecurity and an escape from reality for some. I don't think we will have the problems with gangs in the future. . .because of the higher mentality of society today.

Don Tekavec, 17
Uniontown, Pennsylvania

Chapter 6.

Straights and Gays

To Justin Adaise, senior at Chester A. Arthur High School, it had happened two years ago. Two years ago he had made love to his best friend, Bill Jacobs. And two days ago, Bill died of AIDS. Propped in front of the television, Justin stared numbly at MTV. Those two events, fused together by the pain and doubt swirling within him, burned harshly in his mind. He had not made love to Bill two years ago, and Bill did not die two days ago. Both events were happening now in Justin's head, over and over, again and again, to the macabre sounds of the latest pop music, courtesy of MTV. Make love to Bill; Bill dies. Make love to Bill; Bill dies. Make love to Bill; Bill dies. . . . While the tortuous chant repeated for the thousandth time in Justin's mind, he drifted into an uneasy sleep.

The phone rang and jolted Justin awake. He lunged for the receiver. "Hello?" Justin said timidly.

"Is Mr. Justin Adaise there?" a voice asked.

"That's me," Justin replied nervously.

"I'm calling from the clinic. The results of your test are negative."

Negative! The test results are negative. He is free. He is safe. Justin gave out several joyful screams. He danced on the kitchen table and turned cartwheels across the living room. He started a mental list of who to call with the great news. He had been tested for HTLV-III, the AIDS virus, and the test results were negative.

But as he finished his last cartwheel, Justin came to his senses and realized that he couldn't tell anyone the news. Because no one knew about that night with Bill.

It had happened two years ago at a party. Justin and Bill had been close friends for a couple of years, but Justin didn't know that Bill was a homosexual. He had noticed that Bill never went on dates, but he himself had only gone on a few. They were sophomores, and girls were relatively unknown territory. So Justin thought nothing about the absence of girls in Bill's life.

At this particular party, Justin was very buzzed, thanks to several hours of chugging beer with his friends. As usual, Justin had failed to find a girl for himself at the party. They were mostly taken by all the junior jocks and senior studs who wore football jerseys and drove cars. Justin was having a good time anyway. He knew that as soon as he got his driver's license and his upperclassman status, the girls would flock to him like bees to honey. Or flies to shit, as Bill was always sure to tell him.

Winding his way through the party, Justin found Bill sitting in a corner by himself, strumming a guitar he had found. He sat down next to Bill and recited his usual speech about how he had failed to get a woman, how he didn't care because they didn't deserve a guy like him anyway, how things were going to be so much greater next year, and on and on. Bill listened and smiled as he softly strummed the guitar. Bill was the greatest listener in the world. He was the greatest friend in the world, too. Just by the way he listened and smiled softly as Justin rambled on about his problems, Bill would make him feel so much better. And when Justin was in a good mood, Bill could be so much fun that Justin would feel as though he were on top of the world.

Justin thought about how great Bill was and how lucky he was to have him as a friend. He put his arm around Bill and said, "Thanks for listening again, buddy."

"No problem, bud. I'm used to it by now. In fact, I'd have no purpose in life if I couldn't listen to you ramble on about girls. So thanks for giving my life a purpose, Justin," Bill said, cracking a smile.

"You sarcastic bastard," Justin replied, also smiling. "Here's to us, me and you," Justin continued, raising his cup of beer. Bill returned the toast, and they both chugged what was left in their cups. Justin took the guitar and began strumming an old Beatles tune. Bill went to get refills. When he returned, he gave a cup to Justin, sat down, and listened.

Then suddenly, Bill said, "It's so hot and stuffy in here. Why don't we go outside. I can teach you a new song."

Justin agreed, and they walked outside to the backyard. They walked to the woods, a long way from the house, away from the lights and noise of the party. They sat down, and Bill took the guitar from Justin. Instead of playing it, he placed it on the ground.

"I thought you were going to teach me a new song," Justin said.

"I am," Bill replied. "I love you, Justin."

Justin was caught off-guard by Bill's sudden statement. He replied, "I, uh, I guess I love you, too, Bill." He chuckled nervously, trying to ease the awkwardness of the moment. Bill, however, didn't laugh.

"You don't understand, Justin," Bill said. "I love you." Bill reached out to hold Justin's hand. As he did, his hand brushed softly against Justin's thigh. Almost immediately, Justin felt himself becoming erect. His heart was pounding, and his head swam in confusion and shock, not to mention the influence of eight cups of beer. Justin desperately tried to think clearly about what to do, what to say, even what to think.

While Justin's mind reeled, Bill stared at Justin's crotch. He couldn't help himself. The bulge of Justin's erect penis, straining against his Levi's, was clearly visible. Suddenly, Bill's desire overcame his fear. He reached out and began to gently touch Justin. Justin let out an involuntary sigh. With every gentle stroke, Justin's reservations faded. But wait, no, this wasn't right, it had to stop. . .stop. . .stop. With his last ounce of resistance, Justin pushed Bill away. Bill looked up at Justin, then down at the ground.

"I'm. . .I'm sorry, Justin. I had no right to do that," Bill said. He edged away from Justin.

Suddenly, a voice that Justin did not recognize, a voice that he never knew existed, answered Bill. "That's all right, Bill. I'm glad you did," Justin said. He reached and pulled Bill close again. They kissed, and this time Justin felt a hot, passionate shock rush through his body. It was a shock that seemed to last forever until at last Bill entered him and their bodies became one.

After that night, Justin agonized through a long period of soul-searching. Bill knew definitely that he was homosexual, but Justin was unsure of himself. As the year went by, however, his attraction to girls grew while his attraction to men never materialized, and Justin knew for certain that he was heterosexual.

Justin dated more girls the following year, and he started avoiding Bill. He was too embarrassed, too unable to cope with what had happened. He couldn't face Bill. Because they kept their night together a secret, Justin soon convinced himself that it had never happened.

During the middle of his junior year, Justin began dating a girl and they fell in love. She became his girlfriend, and they began going everywhere together. One weekend, when his parents went for a short vacation, Justin had the house to himself. Justin had been going out with Kathy for several months by that time so he invited her to his house. That night, for the first time, he and Kathy made love. When they did, Justin felt a hot, passionate shock rush through his body. It was a feeling he had not known since the night with Bill almost a year ago. When he felt that passion, Justin knew that he truly loved Kathy. And when he felt that passion, he realized that he also truly loved Bill.

The next day, Justin called Bill for the first time in months. They got together that evening and talked all night. By the end of the talk, after a lot of tears and a lot of laughter, Justin and Bill were best friends again. Their love for one another was too strong for them not to be.

Bill told Justin that as he became comfortable with his homosexuality, he dated men more and more. Bill had discovered a lot of homosexuals in the area, both in high school and out of it. Most of them, like Bill, kept their homosexuality a secret because of the hatred and the hostility that could be unleashed by fellow high school students.

Justin understood Bill's private hell. Keeping his dates secret from his parents and friends; enduring endless questions from his friends about why he wasn't going to the prom; listening to endless faggot jokes at parties; hearing endless talk at lunch about how much pussy everyone got over the weekend. And forcing himself to laugh along with the guys when it really hurt him so badly inside that he wanted to cry.

During the next summer, Bill's life seemed to get a little easier. He found a steady boyfriend, and by the start of senior year he had fallen in love with this man. In November Bill discovered he had AIDS. At first, Bill seemed to have only a nagging cold, like something he might have caught at a football game or during a beer-drinking session out in the car on a cold night. But by Christmas break, Bill was afflicted with a deep, hacking cough. He had trouble breathing, and he ran a constant low fever.

Bill fought the disease bravely. He kept his spirits up, kept his grades high, and kept his social life active. Justin spent more time with Bill than they ever had before. He finally met Bill's boyfriend, John. Justin thought John was a great guy. To Justin, John and Bill seemed really to be in love.

Despite his spirit, though, Bill was slowly being destroyed by AIDS. By the first week of April, he had to stay in the hospital. Three weeks later, two days ago, Bill died.

Died. Dead. Bill died. Bill is dead. Justin snapped back into the present. I am free, but Bill is dead, Justin thought. How unfair. Why? Why!

"God damn it! Why? Why is Bill gone? Tell me! Why did you take him? Damn you, why?" Justin screamed at no one in particular and the whole world in general. He shook his fist at the ceiling. He sobbed uncontrollably.

Bill didn't deserve to die from AIDS anymore than anyone else deserved to die from cancer. But he did.

"Why, why?" Justin kept sobbing as he slumped down to the floor. Justin slowly cried himself to sleep. He didn't cry for the loss of Bill the homosexual. He cried for the loss of Bill the human being, Bill the person, Bill his best friend.

The world would always be a little emptier without him. So would Justin's heart.

Erik Landahl

KRISTIN WAIDE
LTHS

National Reactions—Conflicts

When I stepped on the bus to go to the first day of school. . .I noticed the bus was crowded and each seat had two people sitting on it, except a seat with a blond-haired kid. . . . Since that was the only place for me to sit, I took it. . . .

When I got off the bus at the school, some of my friends ran up to me and told me. . ."You were just sitting next to a fag."

Next day when the bus came to my stop, I noticed. . .the blond-haired kid sitting alone. . . . This time I walked by where he was sitting and crowded in another seat.

Saurabh Joneja, 16
Newark, Ohio

A personal friend of mine is gay. He told me, when he was in high school, he couldn't go through a day without being called "faggot" or "sweetheart" by other guys in a ridiculing manner.

Now he sees these guys in gay bars.

To "get back" at them, he walks up to them and says, "Didn't you call me 'faggot' all the time in high school?"

17-year-old female
South Carolina

It makes me utterly sick to my stomach when homosexuals seem to take pride in their ways and practically brag about them. . . . I view homosexuals as very insecure and wanting of acceptance. . . . They try to make excuses to justify their actions and convince you to see their ways.

Christine Stamper, 17
Newark, Ohio

I think homosexuals should be treated with pity and compassion because what they have is an illness. I don't think I'd associate with them that much, but I wouldn't turn away either.

Sandy Ryczek, 17
Smithfield, Pennsylvania

Once there was a rumor about two guys that were caught kissing at a party. As soon as everyone found out, they really alienated the two guys.

17-year-old female
Iowa

Most of my friends think homosexuality is totally disgusting. . . . Seeing these people in the halls together bothers the hell out of me. I can't stand it when they look at you from top to bottom. You don't know what they're thinking. I know one thing, nobody wants this type of people hanging around our school, giving it a bad reputation.

17-year-old female
Newark, Ohio

The thought of finding out a friend was gay would sicken me.

Regina Fotta, 18
Smithfield, Pennsylvania

Straights and Gays

KRISTIN WAIDE
LT#5

People who desire to have sex with their own sex are, in my book, strange. The idea of a man having sex with another man is more or less a joke. If God wanted a man to have sex with man, he would've put Adam in the Garden with another man and maybe another woman.

Billy Mathis, 15
Chicago, Illinois

I know someone who has a gay brother, and he really goes overboard trying to prove he's not like his brother. If someone has a gay member of their family, people usually assume that the rest of the family is "that way."

Well, the guy I know. . .constantly goes around kissing, dancing, and flirting with all girls. But now he has another problem. Now that he hangs around with the girls, he sort of acts like them. Now many people who know him think he's gay too, and it is hard to tell sometimes.

He also hurts a lot of people while he's trying to prove he's not gay. He has a million flings a year, and then to prove that he's "a man," he drops them. The next day he is going out with someone else.

16-year-old female
Illinois

Adults seem to react a lot more negatively toward homosexuals than teenagers do. This is especially stressed by parents. Parents will often consider a gay person as a threat to his/her children. . . .

I have several friends who are homosexual, and I am often considered a "fag" when I'm with my friends. (We are classified as "punks" to most people.) Because of my being a so-called "punk fag," I'm constantly being harassed and beaten, both physically and mentally. . . .

James Stepanek, 17
Lakewood, Ohio

The town I live in is a conservative suburb of Chicago. People aren't really willing to accept many "different" things. . . .

If a homosexual student became known here, there would be troubles galore for him or her. But the friends of the homosexual would be ridiculed just as much around here. . . . I can see it now: "How's your little fag friend? Trying to slip himself the hot beef injection?". . .

Parents wouldn't be much help either. "Now son, your mother and I don't want you to be like him. He has problems."...

Personally, I don't think homosexuality is right, but if a person chooses to be gay, fine. It's his choice.

Brad Blunt, 16
St. Charles, Illinois

If there were a homosexual around here, I would make sure I'd never go around him or it. If I saw him, I would tell him not to try anything with me or anybody else if he wanted to live.

17-year-old male
Washington

I think homosexuality is totally against the nature of life. God condemns homosexuality in the Bible. This type of relationship doesn't help our race go on. It is a relationship for sexual satisfaction.... A direct result of homosexuality is AIDS. It is ruining the lives of many completely innocent people. Little children and adults are dying because of some gay men who are living a life totally against society and biblical teachings. When I hear of a gay who dies of AIDS, I feel no sympathy.

Matt Harrison, 16
St. Charles, Illinois

I have a friend who is a homosexual, but she doesn't know that I know. If this friend did decide to tell me and ask my advice, I would simply tell her to pray...because I know that God can deliver anyone from anything if only they will believe.

Since I have become aware of her situation, I have not seen her lately....I feel uneasy around her—not that I think she's going to try anything, but I just don't understand how someone can feel so natural about something that is so unnatural to me.

17-year-old female
Arkansas

Discussion

Decatur, Georgia
Emory University

When did you come out?

Rodney: There's coming out to yourself, and there's coming out to the world. It takes years to get from coming out to yourself to coming out to others. Usually, people come out to their friends before they come out to their parents. I accepted my homosexuality when I was 14.

I told my mother during a college vacation. I had been out the night before to a gay bar, and we were late getting back. She wanted to know where we were and why it took so long. Normally I would have made up a lie, but I hate lying worse than anything else. So I asked her if she really wanted to know, and I told her exactly where I had been.

She just sat there. Then she said that she had thought for a while that I was gay, but she didn't want to believe it.

Haftan: I first told my best friend and then my parents when I was 16. I had been going out with a guy for some time, and we broke up in the spring of junior year. That put me into a pretty major depression. I decided I couldn't lie about it anymore. I don't like to compromise myself. When I told my mother, she started crying and didn't stop for hours.

At home, the topic never came up again until the day my presence was requested in the psychiatrist's office. I was handed a plane ticket to leave for a while. After I saw the psychiatrist once, I sent my parents to a psychiatrist. It still doesn't come up.

Something that I miss a great deal is the relationship between myself and my family. I see my heterosexual friends chumming around with their fathers. "Let's go out and have a drink," and, "Joe

brought his girlfriend home for Thanksgiving last year." That simply cannot happen in my family. They know that I'm gay; my father and I don't have this heterosexual chumming around. We didn't have that "father-to-son talk" that all my other friends did. We do go out drinking, but we don't go and play with the cocktail waitress. If I were straight, Dad and I might do that.

I don't bring home someone I'm dating. It's such a normal, healthy, family, American thing to do. "My girlfriend's coming over for dinner. She's going to meet the parents. It's going to be real tense, but it's great." It's very uncomfortable.

My parents didn't let go of any financial support, and they didn't let go of any emotional support. They do not acknowledge my homosexuality. They do not promote its development in any way. I don't think they'd be interested in including my lover in the family.

Rodney: My parents don't like to meet my friends. Not just bringing them home, but if I see a friend of mine on the street, my mother really doesn't want to know. There are a few rare exceptions. My roommate's mother is so accepting. Bill can go up to visit her in New York, and they'll go see a gay-related play on Broadway. She'll introduce him to her gay friends, and she makes jokes about it—kind jokes and friendly jokes.

How did friends react when you told them you were gay?

Rodney: My brother-in-law was upset because I hadn't told him earlier. He had all these friends that he could have introduced me to and lots of questions that he wanted to ask a closer member of the family. I've had people say, "I kind of thought so, but I didn't really think anything of it."

Haftan: Out of those first dozen, there were a lot of tears, but no one withdrew support from me. Friends become very protective. If they hear that someone called me a fag, they get very upset about it. They're like, "Oh, I can't believe it." Or they're like, "Well, who was it?" They become very comforting.

After people who don't know I'm gay have met me, someone will tell them, "Haftan's gay." Then they'll say, "But Haftan's such a nice guy." If someone asks me about my roommate, I'll say, "Yeah, he's straight, but he's an okay guy."

Sometimes people will say, "Haftan, you're gay? You'd never know." Am I supposed to take that as a compliment? The unsaid line behind that is, "Haftan, I know that you want to run home, rape children, and put on dresses. But you're doing a good job of playing it straight." It upsets me.

I've had friends who have known me for ten years come up and say, "Are you still gay, Haftan?" And I'm like, "Are you still straight? Did you change your mind?" They go, "Ooohhhh, I never thought it worked like that."

How did you react when you found out you had gay friends?

Deborah: I found out that my roommate and my two neighbors were gay. I didn't know, and this was halfway through second semester. It scared me because I didn't know how to deal with it. Who could I turn to? I know no other gays except for them. Part of me was angry because they hadn't told me. There was outrage: "Oh my God! How can you be gay? You must be crazy!" When they weren't fitting into any stereotypes, it scared the shit out of me.

Then I realized, "Well, what if they had told me? How would I have dealt with that?" In a sense, they cared enough about me to protect me and to compromise some of who they were to protect me. They really watched out for me.

At that point, I began working through my beliefs. "My gosh. These are my friends whom I've dealt with all this time. These are people who care and with whom I have had a relationship. How can I think of them as being bad when I've seen so much good in them?"

Before last year, if I had known Rodney was gay, I would have run shitless because I couldn't see him as a human being. I would have seen him as a stereotype of a homosexual and that would have made him threatening. Now I see Rodney as the partier, the student, the compassionate friend, everything except he sleeps with men.

Homosexuals threaten a person because they make one look into their own sexuality and say, "Who am I?" I had to do a lot of soul-searching of my own heterosexuality. People are so insecure in their own heterosexuality. My homosexual friends are much more stable people because they know who they are as people. If people would begin to explore more of what sexuality is in heterosexual terms as well as in homosexual terms, perhaps there would not be the fear of homosexuality.

Jeff: I first started meeting homosexuals when I was 16. Previous to that I would have said, "Oh, they're weird." I met all these people, and some of them fit certain factors of the stereotype. Some of them were very effeminate. I just said, "Well, they're nice people. I like them." And then as the years went on, it seemed like a good percentage of my friends were gay. I don't think about it as being abnormal. It's just how my friends are. They're just like anybody else.

How do you tell people?

Rodney: I always like to establish a relationship before I let them know, but I try to keep a little distance. You're always wondering how

they're going to react. Are they going to be very negative or very supportive? Is it someone who's going to get up and yell and scream and leave me at the table very embarrassed?

Haftan: Before I told someone, I would sit preparing myself to never talk to this person again: "I've been in school with this kid for eight years. I've got to go through all this as if he died. Whatever he does has got to be better than death. At least I'm prepared for it." That puts you through hell, especially with close friends and parents.

I don't have such an elaborate system. I would say, "Well, next week when we get together, we're going to have a special talk." And if they had no idea, I'd usually drop them some wonderful poetic line, like, "I'm kind of a virgin," or "I'm sort of not straight," and let them play with it for a while instead of saying, "I'm gay." Those two words can floor anyone.

I take them on this roundabout story, like "Remember when we were at the store yesterday, and we saw this waiter?. . ." Usually the friend is close enough so they're like, "Let me have another drink, and then we'll talk about it." Then as the weeks go by they have more and more questions.

It always comes back to honesty: "This is the way I am." And it always comes down to this idea: If they can't accept homosexuality, then I don't want to depend on them. In some ways, it's the test of, "Can we continue?"

Rodney: Coming out in high school depends on the situation and your parents. Unless the person is very close to their parents and the parents are very liberal, I would not suggest that they tell them. I think coming out is a lot more difficult in high school because you have to see them and deal with them every day.

Haftan: You're very dependent on them. They can kick you out, right

Mandik 87

then and there. I didn't go to my high school prom because I didn't want to show up with a girl, and I knew I couldn't show up with a guy. That pissed me off. You have to weigh it out. If not telling them tears you apart, then you've got to tell them. The only advice I have above and beyond everything else is, have friends you can depend on. My closest friends said, "If you do get kicked out of the house, come right over. As a matter of fact, I can be at your place in case anything happens." Friends have pulled me through everything. They are better than therapists, better than family.

Why is it important for gays to come out?

Haftan: There is a prejudice which was formed long ago. AIDS makes it even worse. There's a greater responsibility for homosexuals to demonstrate that we're everywhere and that we're just like everyone else. Otherwise, it would be very easy to start closing down bathhouses. Why not close down gay apartment buildings? We're in a real unstable period right now. This is the most important time to come out, but it's also the most dangerous.

If you come out of the closet, you become a role model. I'm glad to go over to someone's house, if he just came out. After dinner he'll tell his parents, "Haftan's gay." They're like, "Well, I thought he was such a nice person."

It's so easy to feel like you're the only homosexual in the world. It's so easy to become very depressed or to feel that you're wrong and evil, especially if you've been going to church all your life. You can't go to anyone about it. Growing up, it's very easy to look at your father, the guy down the street, or someone in school who did something related to heterosexuality. But I couldn't go up to my father and say, "Gee, Dad, what did you do at this point?"

If you're absolutely normal, adolescence is bizarre. Try being one of the abnormal. I hadn't been able to start to develop emotionally, socially, or sexually until I started dating other guys.

Deborah: We need people whom one could look up to and say, "He is such a neat person, yet he's gay."

Rodney: The only gay person I knew was a transvestite who lived across the street from my grandmother. I knew I wasn't a transvestite. The way I compensated for that was to read a lot. Whenever there was an article about homosexuality, I read it.

Haftan: If Rock Hudson would have come out long ago, before he died. Or Billie Jean King.

Deborah: Or Martina Navratilova. How can you look at these people and say, "They're crazy and psychotic and they're weird"? You can't! They're perfectly normal people who are homosexual. When I found out that a lot of my friends were gay, I said, "They're supposed to be psycho. They're supposed to be crazy. And they're supposed to be weird." But these are very normal people with very together lives.

How does a person's homosexuality affect social life in high school?

Rodney: I had a steady girlfriend because I didn't want people to think that I was gay. But at parties, I wouldn't go after the girls. I still had a good time with my straight friends in high school even though most people didn't know. I ended up having a lot of contacts and relationships with a lot of different people who got to know me as a person, not necessarily as a homosexual. One of my best friends in high school was gay, and most people ostracized him.

It's interesting to have people who don't think that I'm gay come to me and talk to me about gay people. A lot of gay people tend to

get the concept that everything is all right in the world because gays either associate with other gay people or with heterosexuals who are very understanding.

Haftan: I had a girlfriend in high school, but I'd only see her during football games when everyone was watching. When classes were over, I excluded myself socially to protect myself.

How does a person's homosexuality affect friendships?

Haftan: When it comes to friendships, homosexuality becomes a retardation process. The worst thing you could say to a friend was, "Gee, I'm a cocaine addict," or, "I'm an alcoholic." Things that would be shocking, but that you could deal with. But it's real hard to tell someone you're gay. Most friends knew me for months before they found out. But if people find out that I'm gay before they get to know me, then I run into trouble because I'm battling stereotypes.

I have a close friend. He's straight, and I'm not. I hadn't seen him in a long time. He got off the plane, and he gave me a hug like I would hug my mother or father. When he left, he gave me a kiss on each cheek, very traditional, and thought nothing of it. The people around us froze. He was just expressing his friendship that we've had for so long. No one was capable of understanding that it could just be friendship.

There have been so many instances when it would be so appropriate to express simple emotion. I'll give someone a little punch on the cheek, or something that is typical, and sometimes they'll say, "What are you doing?" "Just giving you a little tap. Ease up. It's okay!" But it's not okay. It all goes back to the stereotype.

Rodney: It's difficult for my mother to accept that I'm a homosexual because she knows no other homosexuals. She just automatically assumes I'm some pervert. I keep pointing back to all the good things that I've done, and saying, "No, mother. I'm not. I'm still the same person who did all these good things in high school and is doing good things now in college."

I have a friend whose sister does not like homosexuals. The friend is very supportive of me. She fusses at her sister for saying bad things about us. She's trying to educate her sister to see that we're all just people.

Haftan: My roommate is having some trouble with his family. He's straight, and his family has just found out that I'm gay. And some of the family members are dealing with it, but they're all sort of looking at him kind of funny. "Why didn't you tell us? Why are you living with him?"

Deborah: I have to admit to some paranoia about being seen with these people. Some of my friends dress flaming, so are people going to think that I'm gay? Because I lived with a homosexual roommate, did people in my dorm think I was gay? Because most of my friends were homosexual last year, did people think I was gay? It does bother me.

Haftan: That's a big fear I have now with my roommate. I've lived with him for two years, and I would feel terrible if I thought that women were avoiding him because they thought he was gay.

Jeff: For a while, so many people thought I was gay that I was beginning to think that I was gay. It was something I got used to eventually. Actually, something that bothers me in relationships with lesbians is not being able to have a sexual relationship if I feel very attracted to them.

Deborah: I've found the same thing. One of my lesbian friends had a big thrill out of telling me that all these guys that I thought were so cute and so sweet were gay. It's pretty heart-wrenching.

Jeff: At the same time, that can also be really good. Because some of my best friends are lesbians, I can just be friends with them.

Haftan: I'm led to believe that my relationships with females are very different from my straight friends' relationships with the same girls. Sex is out of the question, but it's not out of the question with any two heterosexual people. With me and another girl, so much static isn't there.

What are the occupational dangers for gays?

Haftan: I'm pretty much out of the closet now, and it's very difficult to go back in without repercussions. It would be impossible in my major, psychology. I don't know what will happen getting into grad school. It might be on my transcript. Or if they read my work, they might figure it out. God knows I probably can't get a position in a mental hospital.

Deborah: You'd rape all the men, of course!

Haftan: Yeah. I'm left with a private clinic, and I'll see if I can find one where they would know and where it would be okay, because no matter where I am, they're likely to find out. I know I'll lose a job somewhere because of it. Or I won't get a position somewhere. My name won't come up for a promotion somewhere.

Rodney: Being black, there are several things that I'm used to not having and several opportunities that I will not get. By being gay, it's just another thing that's in my way. My parents used to always tell me, "You're just as good as the next person." It's kind of ironic that my mother has come and told me that I'm a second-class citizen now that she knows I'm gay.

What causes homosexuality?

Rodney: Being homosexual is something in you when you're born. Whether you allow expression of that is from environment.

Haftan: I fall back on a biological origin because it makes things simpler. I don't want to look at my past and look for a behavioral pattern. I don't want to look at myself and say, "Oh yes, I must have been seduced and molested as an infant." It is easiest to just start with, "This is how it is."

There comes a point when someone reaches a level of sexual awareness. A guy notices some sort of special feeling when his teacher walks into the room. For me, it was a male, whether it was my fifth grade gym teacher or the guy my sister was dating when I was in twelfth grade. I saw my awareness developing parallel to my heterosexual friends. It wasn't just one day I said, "Well, I used to like women. Today I think I'll start liking men."

People look at me and say, "Well, you just haven't met the right girl." I've explored my heterosexual tendencies. I made a few nice tries. It doesn't upset me that I haven't been able to enjoy sex with a woman. I don't find it distasteful. It's just I know where my enjoyment lies. I'm more convinced of my homosexuality than most people are of their heterosexuality.

How does being gay affect a person's religious viewpoint?

Rodney: I'm presently a deacon at the chapel. I am a strong believer in God, and I am a strong disbeliever in the idea that homosexuals are going to hell. I do not believe that God would have created homosexuals knowing that they would go to hell. There were two distinct references to homosexuality in the Bible, and they weren't good. I think that in a book as large as the Bible, with only two references of

DAN O'BRIEN
LTHS

three verses each, it couldn't be such a big sin.

Deborah: Because churches said, "Being gay is sinful," my friends turned away from the church. They said, "Hell, that's the way I am. If they're not going to accept me, why should I accept religion?"

What type of hostility do gays encounter?

Rodney: The expression is verbal. Walking down the hall of the dormitory, I happened to hear a girl mention my roommate. Everyone in the room started laughing. The girl said, "Well, how do you know that he's gay?" They started laughing again.

Haftan: You can find the most conservative, horrifying groups on campus. Try a fraternity. Try certain departments. It's night and day sometimes. And the difference is a door or a room.

It's easy to say, "You fag." To call someone a Jew. Or a nigger. It's a victory because that word has so many connotations that "you are all of those things, and therefore you are not as good as I am." Even my roommate, who knew I was gay, said, "You fag." I just looked at him and went, "Yes. We know that now. Congratulations. Where do you want to go from there?" He realized that there wasn't a rhetorical victory.

Deborah: People are scared to death. One thing that people fear more than anything is not knowing. It is taught that homosexuality is bad—there's something psychologically wrong with a person who is a homosexual. They're presented as an offensive person, as a drug addict, or as a total psychotic.

How can people end the fear of homosexuality?

Haftan: Try acknowledging homosexuals' presence. I have yet to see ads that really deal with homosexuality openly. If they cater to homosexuals, it's vicarious. We must acknowledge the presence of this population.

Deborah: I grew up in a small town where when you thought of homosexuals you thought of the painted media image. When you deal with people like Rock Hudson or your next-door neighbor's son, then you have to deal with, "This is a normal person, a person you respect who has feelings and emotions." You have to deal with this person on a one-to-one level.

I was able to accept homosexuals because I wasn't being faced with these creatures who wore dresses and were very effeminate, who molested children, or who were psychotics. I was dealing with human beings who had emotions and who dealt with normal problems. Once you see them as normal people who differ only in sexual partners, they aren't weird creatures.

As more people come out of the closet, people are going to have to deal with homosexuals. They're going to have to read literature about homosexuality. Teachers are going to get questions about it in class.

Is gay rights legislation necessary?

Haftan: I can be arrested for being caught in my own bedroom with my boyfriend. Legally, my landlord can kick me out of rented property in Georgia. It's illegal for me to have sex with another man. If I have a lover for 20 years and die tomorrow, my estate goes to my family. It does not go to my lover, who owns half of everything. His half-ownership is taken away. There are all kinds of stupid laws that keep demonstrating that we're worthless people.

Rodney: There was a case here in Atlanta of a man who was arrested for having a homosexual relationship in his own bedroom with the door closed.

Haftan: My mother came to me and wanted me to pass the family name. And I said I just can't do it. "Well, couldn't you adopt someone? You seem fairly paternal. You're good with kids, and I think you might like raising a kid." Well, legally, I couldn't do it.

Rodney: Somewhere a man who had been married, had attempted to live a heterosexual life, and had had children realized that he was gay. He divorced his wife, and he's with his lover now. And he wanted to keep the children. The court, of course, took them away from him.

Haftan: When I open a bank account, when I get insurance coverage, I would expect that if I'm living with a man, we would have a joint savings account. And if we own a house together, we should be able to get joint coverage for things. But we can't.

Memphis, Tennessee
A private home

When did you accept your homosexuality?

Lee: I accepted it more after I was 18 and able to go to gay bars to meet my own type of people. In high school, I thought I was the only weirdo in the school.

Dorothy: I like men, but I always liked women better. I don't really think of accepting homosexuality. It was easier realizing that there were a lot more like me. I found out by reading and by being around people that I wasn't the only one. You might not ever have sex with anyone, but you might still be gay as far as what your preference is. You just wouldn't be active as far as the sexual part.

I know some women who never even consider being with men. And then there's women like myself. If Lee and I broke up, who knows who I would love the next time? Probably a woman, because I'm more comfortable with that. But maybe I would love a man. I have before. It depends on the individual. I think people should just love whom they love.

Lee: I know women who are married who have flings with women. I can't agree with that because they're not being faithful to the one they're with.

Dorothy: Some women might love a man but want to have sex with a woman. But if you really want to live the whole gay life-style, then it would be like Lee and me really loving each other emotionally and physically. I guess it's the same with straight people too.

What makes a homosexual decide to come out of the closet?

Dorothy: She wants to be her way. If straight people want to announce to the world whom they love and whom they want to marry, why should homosexuals not do the same? Why should you have to hide what your feelings are from anyone?

Lee: They're tired of being oppressed, hidden, and held back from everything else.

Dorothy: It's important for gay people not to be silent anymore. If people just go on and live like it's a normal thing, then eventually everyone will feel like it's a normal thing. You're doing a disservice if you hide it. Friends come down to visit us, and they can't stand that we're so open. It embarrasses them. They're so used to hiding it. Why do they want to go work in a straight place, go to a straight bar, act straight, and then go home and love each other? If they were married to a man, they would go out and show it to everybody. But they love each other.

Lee: I don't see how their straight friends couldn't know it. Friends know it. They just don't say anything. Why hide it? You're only

lying to your own self. You'll never be happy with yourself.

Dorothy: Should straight people not put it in the newspaper when they're getting married? That's like saying, "When you get engaged, please don't put your picture in the newspaper saying who you're going to be married to." That's really an injustice for straight people to ask such a thing. I don't ask the people next door not to hug and not to kiss each other in front of me because I'll be repulsed. It's not fair for straight people to say that we should not be blatant. Straight people are the most blatant people there are. The sexual acts of straight people might disgust me, but I'm not going to put that on them so why should they put their inhibitions on me?

I don't think my life is any different than it was when I was married to a man. Just the legal aspect—I can't legally be married to Lee. I can't be on her insurance, and she can't be on mine. If she gets put in prison, I can't visit her as a wife. Or in the hospital.

What causes homosexuality?

Lee: I don't think there's a cause. It's not a disease. You either are, or you're not.

Dorothy: What causes you to be sexual? People want to say it's environment, but I know that's not true. Having all straight teachers, I didn't end up being straight. I don't think it has anything to do with environment.

If everyone would quit thinking of it as a fault or a disease and just get comfortable with it, then it would be a lot different. Who knows why anyone's gay or why anyone's heterosexual?

Lee: My family definitely says they don't understand it. They don't accept it, and they never will. For years they looked at it as putting up with me while I put up with them. And why should I? I've got my life

to live, and I'm finally living it. Either they love me or they don't. Either I'm their daughter or sister, or I'm not.

Why do people harass homosexuals?

Dorothy: They've got to pick on somebody! Not knowing, and a fear of being one yourself and not being accepted.

Lee: They don't understand it. It's just a phobia that they have. The Ku Klux Klan picks on blacks. It's just something to harass somebody about.

Do you think it's more difficult being gay in the South?

Lee: It's easier being gay here. When I was in the Army, there was one club around that we could go to. We could come and go as we pleased, which we've been able to do for the last 10 or 12 years that I've been out.

Dorothy: Memphis is pretty open-minded about that. Every city probably has places that are liberal, but maybe the suburbs are more conservative. When you're living in the heart of a city, then you've got all types of people. You can't really live there if you're going to be close-minded. You wouldn't survive very long.

Lee: I think increased media attention is helping more people to become aware that we're here.

Dorothy: It's good. Even the negative is good. But the only thing that is really bad is that the writing is discriminatory. But even so, it's good because it brings attention. It lets everybody know it's not going to go away. It's not something they can just forget about and think we're going to all change or hide.

Lee: AIDS is going to slow us down a little bit, but I don't think it's the gay people's problem.

Dorothy: It may be a gay men's issue. Definitely lesbians do not have AIDS so how can you say it's homosexual when half of the homosexual segment does not have AIDS? But it just happens that the way that men have sex, that's the perfect environment for the virus. That's also not the only way you can get it. AIDS has made it hard for gays because more people are afraid. It used to be that they just didn't want to hear about it, but now they're kind of scared.

Tucson, Arizona
A local high school

What causes homosexuality?

Sabrina: Gays are people who have been rejected. They feel that the only kind of love they can get is from their own sex. They've never had any other experience with people who make them feel happy.

What makes you think someone is gay?

Shannon: Tight jeans.

Sabrina: The men are just kind of "swishy," and they come across as if they're all haircutters. Women work on construction and cars. Or a girl who may look like a "butch"-type person.

Aloysias: There can be a homosexual who's 6'4", weighs about 250 pounds, and is all muscle. You never can tell unless you're

approached or you see two homosexuals interacting sexually.

We should treat them like anybody else as long as they're not harming us or harming our morals or values. I don't think they should be discriminated against because of what they do in their lives as long as they show others respect. A gay person could be a microanalyst, making $300,000 a year, and I could be straight and digging ditches.

I've been approached before, and I've dealt with it. I wasn't rude or anything, but I just said, "Man, I don't fuck around with other guys." He understood that. I was kind of nervous because that had never happened to me before, but it was an interesting experience to be approached like that.

Rachel: You could say, "Oh, I think society should just treat them like any other people, but if you're in a room and somebody says, "Everyone else in this room is gay," you could freak out.

Sabrina: The only thing that bothers me about homosexuality is that AIDS is a major issue. That's what's scary about it. I read this article that these men have 40 interactions a night at these homosexual parties. You don't know who you get AIDS from. There's no cure for it. You just die. People have a hard time dealing with gays because they think that they're the ones who carry AIDS.

Vaughne: I think people are afraid of homosexuals. People usually think that all gays are disgusting.

Sabrina: I don't think they're mature enough to deal with it. It's also not macho for a guy to think that it's okay for a person to be gay. Women are the same way. It's just not normal, but who says anything's normal?

Is it possible to be friends with someone who is gay?

Rachel: It's possible. If you really think about it, you say, "Hey, this person's my friend, and I like this person." If the friendship is really strong, it will overcome the fact that he or she is gay. A friendship is stronger than sexual preferences.

If a friend told you he or she were homosexual, how would you react?

Sabrina: I'd probably be shocked because, I mean, if I had been working with them for so long. And I'd probably think, "Oh my God. Is she looking at me in a certain way?" But if she's your friend, and you have been normal friends for a long period of time, then it shouldn't matter. As long as you know that she's not going to make any interactions with you.

Mark: I worked at Carlos Murphy's, and there was a waiter there. You couldn't even tell that he was gay. One day we were eating lunch together, and he goes, "Did you know I was gay?" I was shocked, but we talked about it. They understand that people who aren't don't want to be approached. They respect that, and they want you to respect the way they feel.

Shannon: You aren't going to think about them the same. You'll be wondering what he's thinking and the way he's looking at you.

Sabrina: I'm sure that you'd get over it. Let's say that you've been friends with someone for ten years and all of a sudden the person tells you that he or she decided to come out of the closet. It shouldn't matter. You have to be mature enough to deal with it. You're going to be shocked, but you can get over it easily. It doesn't involve you. It's his or her preference.

Shannon: When you found out that that guy was gay, afterwards were you the same way you were before you knew he was gay?

Mark: No, I was different because he used to look at me. He used to give me an extra share of the tip. But he was a nice guy. He never tried to do anything. I was always thinking, "The guy's gay," but it didn't come between our friendship. It wasn't that strong of a friendship, but I still ate with him and I still talked to him.

Vaughne: When you hear someone's gay, nothing can stay the same. But you've got to deal with it. You've got to tell yourself, "This person is still the same person that he was before, but I know something else about him now." And maybe your attitude may change somewhat, but I don't think it should affect the friendship.

Rachel: If you're friends with someone for ten years, chances are you're going to know.

Should people hide their homosexuality?

Vaughne: It depends on them— whether they feel that they can trust you and whether they feel that you can handle it.

Mark: If they feel comfortable about telling you, they should. Like, that guy must have felt comfortable about telling me.

Is homosexuality a sin?

Mark: God didn't put Adam and John on earth. He put Adam and Eve.

Vaughne: If he can create Adam and Eve, why can't he create a guy and a guy at that time? How do you even know that there's an Adam and Eve?

Ken: If everyone were a homosexual, we wouldn't be here right now.

Vaughne: He put Adam and Eve on earth so we could reproduce. I don't think that He would do it just so we could discriminate.

Rachel: Maybe that's true, but who said it was a sin to begin with? Just because God didn't put another man on earth doesn't mean it's sinful.

Ken: No, he put them on earth to make kids so the world could keep on going.

Aloysias: As far as a sin is

concerned, hitting a cow could be a sin. It depends on your religion and your outlook on life. Everyone has a different opinion about whether it is a sin. I really can't answer the question because I don't know enough about it to judge it. I just know it's not for me.

Vaughne: I remember watching "Saturday Night Live" one time when the Rolling Stones were on. Mick Jagger licked Keith Richard's face, and it was just so disgusting. But people didn't care because the Rolling Stones are just so big and they have so many hits.

Ken: At University High, you see girls walking around holding hands.

Ron: They could have kept to themselves. If they want to do it, that's their problem but not in front of everybody. And in high school, it's just yuck. The principals kicked them off the school grounds.

Sabrina: I can handle seeing two guys doing that more than two girls. I was in France with my family, and these two girls were getting really into it. I was so grossed out. I couldn't believe it. I can handle seeing two guys. When I was skiing, I saw these two guys kiss on a chairlift in front of me. It didn't surprise me as much.

Mark: There was a guy who dressed really weird. He came to school in a dress, and they made him walk home. They walked him off the school grounds. That was for his personal well-being because some guys would probably go up to him and kick his, you know.

Sabrina: I felt bad because people were surrounding him and stuff. He had to either prove something or show people that he's different. He had to get so much crap from everyone.

Ron: The kids were worried about the image of the school. They have friends from other schools saying, "Hey, you go to that school? They've

got fags running around there." That's what a lot of students are worried about. That's why they prefer that the gays get out.

Vaughne: My dad is always going, "Oh my God. We have to move. There's a faggot sitting by us." He got on the topic, and he kept saying "Faggot, faggot, faggot." He comes from a very small town, and the people there are very small-minded. I don't think that someone should be saying that. I believe that whatever someone wants to do, it's up to them, I asked my parents what would happen if my brother or I ever told them we were gay. They said that they would just feel sad for us because we couldn't have children or a family.

New York City
New Youth Connections office

Carlos: It's gotten to the point now where even if your friends are gay it's like so what?

Penny: Before a couple of years ago, you would have been afraid. But now, ever since this Harvey Milk School, so many teenagers admit that they're gay.

Misha: The only reason that they have to be scared is AIDS.

Can you tell by looking at a person if that person is gay?

Felix: It depends on how flamboyant the person is, whether he acts like a woman. Or if it's a woman, whether she acts like a man.

Misha: You can't go up to anybody, look at them, and tell if they're straight or not. I don't see how you could tell whether they're gay.

Carlos: You can see it in the street. Two guys holding hands looking very feminine. You'd be kind of shocked if they're straight.

Keith: You might think in some Latin American cities that all men

are gay because there's so much physical affection between straight men.

Penny: I've seen men who are straight wearing skirts so you really can't even go by the clothes they're wearing.

Carlos: Acceptance of gays may have to do with us living in the city. Out in the suburbs, gays are going to be lynched within five minutes.

What causes homosexuality?

Felix: It's genetic mutations. It's just changes that occur in the genes. It's something that's different from all the other species.

Carlos: No, it's not genetic. It's just the way you are.

Felix: You like girls. Your friend may like guys.

Penny: And what causes girls to like guys?

Misha: Some guys feel closer to their father so they might look for

male affection. The same holds for girls and their mothers.

Felix: I read in a book that gays have more affection for their mothers so they wouldn't do it with a woman because they feel that it's their mother.

Penny: That's like saying a child who just lost a father will marry a man 20 years older, looking for a father and marriage.

Misha: Suppose they just lived with their father. That was the only affection they got. So then I think, "This is the right way. This is the way I was brought up so this is the correct way."

Penny: I read an article by a homosexual man. He said he was gay because his father was never around and was always yelling at him. He wanted male affection. That's why he turned out to be homosexual.

Carlos: But you can't say what really caused it because in different people it's different things. You can't say why you like pizza but you don't like hamburgers.

Keith: Obviously, human beings have the capacity for affection, both between sexes and among sexes, so you might think, "What prevents it?" It seems odd that men who can have very close relationships with other men but can't express that sexually feel they can with a woman. So is there some very strong social taboo that prevents something that they would do naturally?

It could be biological. Males and females are so attracted because it results in procreation. It makes good sense for that to be really strongly genetically programmed. Otherwise we would die out.

On the other hand, there's nothing to lose genetically by being a homosexual. A man has the capacity to father hundreds and hundreds of children—thousands in a lifetime. He has nothing to lose having homosexual experiences as long as he has heterosexual sex a few times. The same with a woman. She has the capacity to have sex all day long and every day of her life. She only needs to have sex with a man a couple of times to pass on her genes.

Carlos: What causes homosexuality is what's in the person's head. Why would some black guy go out with white girls? Why would some white girl go out with Chinese boys? It's their preference. So a man has the preference to be with another man. That's his right.

What makes a homosexual decide to come out of the closet?

Misha: Maybe they're tired of hiding it. After a while you just have to tell somebody. You can't hold it in.

Penny: They have to pretend they're straight at work. At lunch with other guys, they're talking like, "Yeah, I had this girl this weekend." Inside, it's eating them up because they have to live a lie.

Carlos: It's really self-respect. I mean, you don't want to walk around with a bag over your head. You want to be accepted for who you are.

What would you do if your child told you he was gay?

Carlos: I'd tell him, "Sit down, and really think about who you'd rather spend your sexual life with because once you make a decision, chances are you have to stick with it for the rest of your life."

I know a couple of gay guys who told their friends that they were gay. Their friends started saying, "Nah, you can't be gay because you're my friend." They got into fights, but they stood their ground. If you're gay, don't be gay and be a pansy about it. Be gay, and stand up for your rights.

People are going to treat you like shit. It's like when you start a new school for the first time. You're always striving to be accepted by some group but you also have to stand up for yourself.

How do people react when their friend tells them he or she is gay?

Misha: You'd be a little shocked.

The first thing you'd think is, "You're my friend. You can't be gay. I've known you all my life. You don't look gay." In your head you might be thinking, "Oh boy, she spent the night at my house last weekend" and all those things.

Penny: When my friend told me that he was gay, it shocked me. I responded, "You're happy, right?" He said, "I'm gay. I like men." He kept telling me about it, and he started talking to me about his problems. That's the way you accept it. We sit around, and we talk about guys. He tells me his problems, and I tell him mine. He's just one of the girls.

Carlos: If a friend of mine comes up to me and says, "I'm gay," I'm going to give him credit for coming out and saying it. He had the balls enough to come up and tell me.

Lombard, Illinois
Glenbard East High School

What is the stereotype of a homosexual?

Dave: A limp-wristed fag. Have you ever seen the Showtime production "Brothers"? Donald is the stereotypical homosexual. He's got his life together, but he presents himself very effeminately. Very, "Ooh, look at that!" Squirming when a handsome man walks in.

Sue: Very feminine.

Kevin: A woman would be like a lumberjack.

Brad: If you are talking about men, walking around in women's clothing. You expect them to be florists or hairdressers. The stereotype is false. The person I know who's gay is an architect. On the other hand, his transvestite husband is a costume designer for Broadway. They got married in San Francisco.

I was around 13 when I found out. After the surprise, I felt rejection. You don't want to

associate with this person. After seeing the indications of it, I couldn't deal with it. I think it's a loss of respect. What are we going to talk about? What if he starts talking about men?

Kevin: It changes the whole relationship. I had a friend who was, and I couldn't talk to him after I found out. I really respected the person. When I found out, 60 percent of my respect for him was gone. Most people have a fear that they may become homosexual if they associate with homosexuals.

Brad: They'll walk up and proposition you. I've hung around with a friend who's homosexual. His friends will proposition you even if you know them.

Sue: If I found out that my very best friend was a lesbian, I would still hang out with her. I don't base relationships on that. I found out my manager at work was gay. I didn't respect him any less. It was just a fact of life.

My sister dated a guy who was bisexual. He dressed effeminately. He had an effeminate haircut. Lots at guys at U of I wear makeup. That didn't change their relationship. She has a good friend who is homosexual. She loves him because they have so much in common. He's real feminine, and she's real feminine. She knows he's not going to hit on her. They can just hang out.

Meaghan: God created men, and He created women. Biologically, men and women are supposed to be together, not man and man. It's against nature.

Sue: If you're saying that people don't choose to be homosexuals, then you're saying they are born that way. Do you believe that God made them that way? If God says it's wrong, then why is God turning around and making people homosexual?

Pat Meyer (teacher): It probably has a lot more to do with one's

psychology and with how one was brought up rather than whether God inherently made someone homosexual. It seems to draw heavily on the psychological climate of one's house—the overbearing mother, the dependence on the mother, the psychological absence of the father. Some of the homosexual men I know are terrified of women. Often they've had a bad relationship with their mother, and they don't want to have relationships with women.

Boston
Copley Square High School

What is the stereotype of gays?

Peter: Men who act like girls. Women who act like guys.

Rosa: Feminine. They use their hands a lot.

Noel: They wear earrings in both ears, and dresses. They're flexible in their walk.

Xavier: Beard, mustache, baldness, leather jacket, skinny.

What makes people gay?

Eldin: I've heard that a guy has had too much of girls and he wants to get into something new.

Rosa: Gays want to be gays because they feel better as the opposite sex. Suppose I want to be a boy. I go and change my sex because I feel better that way.

How do friends and family react to coming out?

Eldin: I would try to talk him out of it.

Peter: Gays have to think, "Will my parents still accept me?" Friends will be thinking, "You're a faggot, and you might turn me into one." If you hung around them for five years, they would say, "Go, get out of here. Go hang around the girls."

Noel: I know a parent who accepted the child even though he was gay. As long as the child was happy, she was happy. If I were the mom, I'd get him a girl and prove to him he wasn't a fag.

Friends wouldn't accept you. They'd think, "Get away you fag. Don't come on the baseball team. You're not changing in here. Go to the girls' room." God created everyone perfect. If you turn gay, you are making yourself different and that means you are disbelieving in God.

Peter: The Pope and God say that you're not supposed to be gay so I couldn't go to church or live with myself anymore and worship someone I don't believe in. If God doesn't send gays into heaven, then why should we accept them?

Xavier: The way we were made, women and men, it works perfect. If two men have anal sex, it's not right. Sex was given to you, but you're using it the wrong way.

Peter: In my community, gays aren't accepted. The only person who is gay got beat up. People are afraid because some gays will make a pass, try to like you, or talk to you if you walk around them. Around my way, you have to walk through where these gay people live. I take the long way home because I feel uncomfortable.

Should gays be allowed to teach?

Eldin: Gays can teach about fashion because it deals with women, and they know about clothes.

Peter: If a gay teaches science or something, then there will be problems. No one will want to talk to him or ask for help.

Eldin: I think gays do not deserve to be treated as people. This whole thing is their problem. They started it. It's sinful. Men and women make babies. God gave gay people AIDS and said, "Okay, you want to be gay, then take this disease. Now you're going to have really big problems. People are really going to be against you."

Peter: Some gays come out because

they feel that's the way they are. They shouldn't feel ashamed of themselves.

Compiled by Greg Jao

Solutions

Adults and adolescents. . .view gays as extreme aberrations of the accepted society. Adolescent reactions may be less severe but more cruel. Teenagers tend to verbally express their obnoxious opinions about gays while adults are more severe by openly shunning and decapitating the gay species. Personally, I think gays should be transferred to Russia and placed in eternal exile in Siberia.

> *Yvonne Hui, 17*
> *Columbia, South Carolina*

"I'm gay" was all she said to me. . . . She is my best friend. I'm supposed to understand. I didn't want to understand anything. I didn't even want to be near "her kind."

One day something changed my mind. I was losing my best friend over something I didn't understand. I went and made her explain everything to me. Her explanation was crystal clear. "I just wanted someone to love me, someone I knew I could trust," she said.

Now I understand "her kind." A little communication helped one person from the younger generation. It might help the older if they just try.

> *17-year-old female*
> *Ohio*

I have a friend who has a preference for males. He's clean. I don't advise him. I let him be free, which is how I feel—free.

> *Kellye Brown, 16*
> *North Little Rock, Arkansas*

A friend of mine had a personal experience with . . . a homosexual. . . .

"Jim" made a pass at my friend, and my friend got really pissed off. I always treated Jim as a human being, and I always will. If God loves everyone just the way they are, who are we to judge? . . .

I don't agree with homosexuality. . . . It is really gross. But . . . after all, society is full of things we must adjust to or we'll be the outcasts. Homosexuality is something I've . . . adapted to. You just can't ignore it and expect it to go away.

> *18-year-old male*
> *Pennsylvania*

I have met two gay guys. . . . I saw and talked with both of them. When they left the room, my friend ran over to me and asked me if I knew they were gay. I went into shock. . . . I got sick at the thought.

I didn't want to touch them or anything they had touched. I . . . talked about it with my parents, and they were like, "Don't you ever, ever go around them again." "You can get AIDS," was my dad's first response.

I kept my distance from them for about a week, then finally realized they were my friends, and maybe I should talk to them about it.

I did, and now I understand things more clearly.

> *Jessie Wood Lucas, 18*
> *Trenton, Kentucky*

If somebody liked vanilla and you liked chocolate, would you hate that person? Of course not.

> *17-year-old male*
> *Pennsylvania*

For a long time, it was minorities being discriminated against. Now it's homosexuals. . . . The situation is the same—they get treated just like us minorities. For any species other than white, it is hard to find a good job or apartment. You can't walk in public without someone saying, "Yuk, look at that———."

Well, I have news for all the people like this—you're no better. In fact, homosexuals and minorities have a slight edge because we know that we have to try even harder to be successful. I'm not for homosexuality nor. . . against it. I just think that everyone should be given a fair shot.

Juan Cepe, 19
Newark, Ohio

If you like somebody of the same sex, that's okay. People are human, and you can't help what you feel, as long as no sexual activity is involved. Then it's wrong. Sexual activity in humans can be controlled. But what's wrong with liking all kinds of people, male and female?

Jamie Bafico, 16
Stockton, California

We should treat homosexuals as freaks because if God wanted men to have sex with men, there would be no women. . . . But He made two sexes so gay people don't belong in our society. Maybe they should get on a boat and go to another country and start their own society like the Pilgrims did.

Bryan Greene, 18
Uniontown, Pennsylvania

They should put a homosexual in a dark corner and leave him there. They should beat someone that is homosexual. Then lock him up with about 500 naked women until he straightens up, or he dies in the process.

18-year-old male
Pennsylvania

I was shocked to find out that my friend was a homosexual, but then I realized that it did not make a difference. If I never. . . found out, I would still think of them highly. How could finding out make a difference now?

Sometimes I think it would have been better if I didn't find out in the first place. But the problem is not too hard to handle. . . .

Lisa Fink, 15
St. Charles, Illinois

The reactions of adults and teens toward homosexuals are less different than people think. We teens have our radical ways to deal with the problem of homosexuals, such as electrocution and other methods of torture. While adults outwardly disapprove of our way of thinking, I imagine they love our ideas. Who wants a homosexual spreading AIDS or any other venereal diseases? I don't like it, and neither does the majority of the American people.

Adults have shown their dislike for homosexuals by discriminating against them in the job market and the housing industry. Teens can't discriminate against homosexuals in the same way as adults, but we have our ways. Homosexuals. . . are mercilessly taunted by "normal" students and must stay in their own group and away from us, the normal students. . . .

It's refreshing to see adults and teens band together and fight against something that is hurting our country. Maybe our togetherness will control the homosexual problem in America today.

16-year-old male
Ohio

Straights and Gays

Chapter 7.

Nonhandicapped and Handicapped

A familiar feeling of discomfort crept down my spine as I looked at my cousin's short, chubby figure and moonlike, fleshy face. I caught a glimpse of her wide tongue through her open, slack mouth. Her slanted eyes above the short nose were seeking mine, staring, as if she were reading my eyes. Awkward even with little children, I was totally at a loss around an adult with the mentality of a preschooler. I tried to ignore the sinking feeling in my stomach, and forced enthusiasm into my smile and voice.

"Faye, you look great!" She shifted her feet and held up her arms. I bent awkwardly to give her a hug; I had to stop myself from pulling immediately away.

"Hi, Kelly," she said in her slow voice, which made everything she said sound profound. She looked at me expectantly. I racked my brain for something suitable to say.

"How are you doing, Faye?" I asked seriously, as if I really wanted to know. I struggled to sound cheerful and to look interested. I tried to produce meaningful replies to Faye's proud recital of accomplishments. My aunt and uncle added tidbits to spur Faye on while my parents exclaimed appropriately.

"Kelly. . . I've got a job," she said importantly as she shifted her weight from foot to foot.

"A . . . a job, Faye? How could. . . I mean, um, really? How great! What do you do?" Embarrassment burned through my body. I ducked my chin in an attempt to hide my glowing face, but I forced myself to lift it again so Faye wouldn't think I was ignoring her. I avoided anyone's eyes except Faye's.

Faye sucked her tongue forward while she thought, as if she had a bad taste in her mouth. Chewing her cud, I thought. She shifted her weight while her eyes searched the floor. Then she looked to her mother for help.

"Faye works in a factory, isn't that right, Faye?" my aunt prodded.

"Yes. . .I cap bottles." Faye's eyes gleamed with pride.

"Wow! Faye! How exciting!" my mom gushed, her body convulsed with enthusiasm, her face twisted with animation.

Faye beamed.

"That's really great, Faye. Good for you!" I echoed.

"She pulls the lever for every load of Fizz-Up on her assembly line. They're a small, local factory that hires a lot of handicapped people," my aunt added confidentially. "The school she went to last year tries to help them find community jobs they can handle. And you fit right in, don't you, honey?" My aunt patted Faye on the shoulder. Faye gazed complacently into space.

"Tell them about the bonus you earned last month," my uncle encouraged.

Goaded by her parents, Faye haltingly told us. She paused, waiting expectantly for our reaction after each sentence. Her eyes searched ours as she continued.

Unsure how to respond to her blatant appeal for praise and attention, I cringed inwardly whenever her eyes found mine. I uncomfortably followed my mother's lead, oohing and aahing as if Faye were a child. That felt wrong, though, because Faye was nearly 25 years old. Feeling awkward and self-conscious, I knew that my repetitive rendition of, "That's great!" and, "How exciting!" and, "Ooh, Faye!" sounded forced.

I couldn't help but wonder if she were aware that we talked to her differently than we talked to "normal" people. I hated treating her like a child—that seemed condescending and rude. Faye was a relative of mine. I loved her, and I wanted to treat her with respect.

I suppressed a sigh of relief when my aunt broke up the conversation by suggesting we all go inside. Hoping for a breather away from Faye, I offered to help my aunt serve drinks, but then my aunt asked Faye to help us carry the tray.

After serving the others, I re-entered the kitchen to see Faye holding her glass as she waited for me.

"I'll have iced tea, please," she said.

"Sure. . .um, no problem," I accepted the glass she thrust at me with her short, thick, wrinkled fingers.

"Do you want ice?" I asked politely. Stupid question, I thought. She asked for iced tea.

"Yes, Kelly." She watched me as I broke ice into both our glasses. She shifted her weight impatiently as I poured the tea.

I carefully handed her the drink. As I followed her into the living room, I noticed once again her slightly waddling, ungainly walk. Faye curled up next to her parents on the couch, and I chose a chair on the other side of the room.

"Faye, your dad's been telling me you have a boyfriend," my mom happily exclaimed.

"His name is Bill," Faye said with a smug look.

"That's right, but you have a couple of other boyfriends, don't you, Faye?" My aunt encouraged her in a go-ahead-don't-be-modest tone of voice.

Faye looked down and shifted her legs, then searched her audience. "Ray. . .he wants to be my boyfriend. And Buddy, he's my boyfriend too." Faye looked even smugger.

"But Bill is your main boyfriend?" my mom asked. Faye smiled uncomprehendingly and didn't answer.

My aunt spoke up. "Yes, Bill is the one she likes the most, but she's popular with just about all the boys. Isn't that right, honey?"

Oblivious, Faye gazed into space.

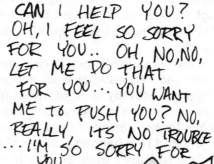

from the
Teen Medical Journal

The Handicap Syndrome:
the symptoms·   the cause·

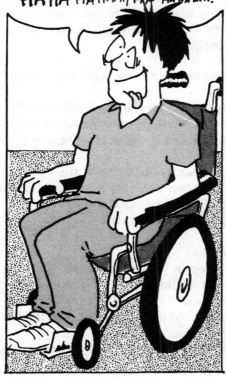

"Did you meet them at work, Faye?" My mom's voice prodded Faye to respond.
"Yes." She glanced at my mom, then continued to gaze at her size three feet.
   "At work, but she also has lots of boyfriends from school. She still writes to a couple of them. In fact, one of them moved to Texas, and he still writes her every two weeks." My aunt stroked Faye's curly hair, and Faye nestled her head against her shoulder.
   "My goodness, Faye! All the way from Texas! He must really like you to write you from so far," my mom squeaked.
   Faye grinned and chortled.

Nonhandicapped and Handicapped   115

"Wow, Faye, you sure know how to keep 'em on a string," I commented lamely.

Faye giggled again as she looked to her parents, who gave her congratulatory smiles. My aunt hugged her.

My aunt rose to her feet. "I'd better start dinner. Why don't you all unpack and get settled now so we can relax after dinner. Faye and Hazel, you show everyone where to sleep."

I followed my cousin Hazel, one year younger than I, to her bedroom upstairs. She said both my sister and I could sleep on the floor in her room, or one of us could sleep in Faye's room. I looked at my sister. I knew we would prefer to sleep in Hazel's room though neither of us wanted to say it in front of Faye.

"I'll sleep here," I said, guiltily plunking my case down and leaving my sister in the ditch.

"Are you going to sleep in my room, Mary?" Faye asked my sister. Faye liked Mary because she had babysat a lot and was good with kids.

"Well. . .actually, a lot of my stuff is in Kelly's suitcase so I really need to be with her so we can share." Mary shot me a half-uncomfortable, half-accusing look.

Faye looked down, shifted her weight a few times, and said, "Oh, okay."

Mary and I exchanged guilty looks. Mary knelt down to face Faye, who looked up, straight into Mary's eyes, only inches away. I could tell it made Mary uncomfortable.

"Do you understand, Faye?" Mary pleaded.

Faye nodded.

"Why don't we go down and play spoons before dinner, huh? Would you like that?"

Faye nodded again, with more energy.

"Let us unpack, and we'll all come down and play spoons. Why don't you go ask your mom what time dinner will be so we know how much time we have?" Mary's eyes followed Faye's figure out of the room. She looked at me, and we both self-consciously looked at Hazel.

Mary and I needed hangers so I went downstairs to check the coat closet in the living room. Passing the kitchen, I saw Faye with her arms around her mother.

"Nobody's going to sleep in my room," Faye complained.

"Honey, that's their decision. Mary said it wouldn't be convenient," my aunt said sternly.

"I wanted someone to sleep with me, too."

"Faye, I'm not going to tell them to sleep in your room so be quiet about it. You knew it wouldn't work anyway because they wouldn't want to go to sleep at eight like you do. They'd wake you up no matter how quiet they tried to be when they came in. Then you wouldn't be able to get up for work. And you'd wake them up getting ready for work. They want to sleep late during the summer."

Faye gave up. She turned to leave the kitchen and collided with me, sneaking past with the hangers.

As we bent down to pick up the scattered hangers, I caught my aunt's eye. Neither my aunt nor I spoke. We didn't need to.

Kathy Segraves

DAN O'BRIEN
LTHS

Nonhandicapped and Handicapped   117

National reactions—Conflicts

I have extreme trouble with handicapped people. . . . I hate them all because they steal my parking spots. My dad says they're just a waste of the taxpayers' money, and I believe him.

17-year-old male
Missouri

MATTHEW HYDE
LTHS

Privileges given to handicapped individuals are many times taken advantage of. . . . There are a few individuals in our student body that do anything they want and the teachers and staff let them get away with it. Physically, handicapped people need more help. . . . But many people push this to the limit. Many will give up and say, "I'm handicapped and unable to do this." They want to be treated like "normal" people, but they won't act like it.

The handicapped should be treated like everyone else except for what their handicap limits them from doing. And it is expected that they should use the facilities that are provided for them if they have the need. But if they do not have the need to use them, they should get along without them like everyone else does.

Lance Palubicki, 16
Hanover Park, Illinois

There are some retarded kids that come to learn. Sometimes we'll see them in the hall, and I'll be walking with my friends. My friends won't say anything until they have left. Then they imitate the way they walk and talk, and they laugh about it.

I laugh with them because what else can I do? It goes with the saying, "What they don't know won't hurt them," but it really does. There is always that one person who isn't afraid to make fun of them while they watch. Then that one person is considered cool, but to me that person is sick.

Linda Wulf, 15
Munster, Indiana

There are a lot of personal conflicts because I'm a profoundly deaf student in a school with 1,400 other hearing students. But I try to keep my handicap out of the conflicts because I hate pity— it is the most dehumanizing thing anyone could offer me.

Deborah Wright, 17
Harper Woods, Michigan

I don't feel any problems are caused by special privileges for the handicapped. If anything, more problems are caused for them by people without handicaps. I happen to know this for a fact because I myself have a handicap. I am visually impaired—legally blind. . . .

I was constantly teased in grade school for the way I read (with my nose an inch away from the paper). Also, people don't always understand the extent of my handicap and sometimes expect more than I'm capable of (but I'll try anyway).

I have also worked with and have been around the mentally retarded. People never give them a chance to prove themselves, or even do anything for themselves. I have seen many people either make fun of them or ignore them.

Julianne Vasey, 15
Arlington Heights, Illinois

Handicapped people in my school and community are treated like kings and queens. They all get out of class five minutes early, and they expect everybody around them to feel sorry for them. If you don't, they'll run you over with their wheelchair or they'll get really mad.

In our community, it's worse. One time around 11:30 P.M. I had to go to Jewel and parked in the handicapped spot. No one else was in the parking lot. I came out, and I had a $50 ticket on my windshield because I parked there—and all the "crips" were in their castles sleeping on their waterbeds.

Not like I hate them, I feel sorry for them (sort of). Whose fault is it? Not mine. Whose problem is it? Not mine. So why do we get their balm every time something goes wrong with them. It's like I'm sorry for what happened to them, but I'm glad it's not me.

Greg Nowak, 16
Munster, Indiana

Handicapped students in my school are treated the same way as any ordinary people. From what I've seen, at least, there are no putdowns or staring or anything like that.

But if I would talk about the whole community, it is very different. . . . Everywhere they go, they get stared at or put down a lot. In school, I've seen a lot of students talking to the handicapped students, but in the city in public, I hardly see anyone walking with them or talking to them.

I think the students in the schools respect them more than people on the streets. Businessmen or women don't go around putting them down, but there are a lot of putdowns coming from people who hang around the streets—who have no respect for anybody. And when I say handicapped, I mean both physically and mentally.

Kathryn Lee, 14
Portland, Oregon

Handicapped are treated as objects of ridicule or abuse. My high school is a ridiculous stereotype in that its average student is a yuppie at a younger age. Imperfection is not something to be tolerated by the rich, the influential, and the stylish.

In my math class, there is a senior who is socially retarded. He doesn't relate well. He annoys the class and teacher with pointless questions, and his personal hygiene is suspect. Students in the class go out of their way to insult, threaten, or embarrass him.

In my community, the handicapped are not part of the Republican uppercrust. They are considered to be the lower, pitiable, "welfare" levels, best fit for misfits and outcasts.

The physically handicapped are accepted only so long as their handicap doesn't affect their image, their appearance. Otherwise, toss 'em out, down with the stoners, geeks and cruds. "We couldn't associate with that kind!"

The attitude is superficial, concerned only with the outer image, not the inner person.

16-year-old male
Indiana

They sometimes feel sorry for themselves and act as if they are different when actually they are not. I feel that everyone in school, handicapped or not, should be accepted and treated as every other person would be.

Christi Hansen, 14
Portland, Oregon

Discussion

*Minneapolis
South High School*

Elaine: I was in a car accident when I was a baby. That's how I became handicapped. When I was 2½ years old, I went into a foster home because my parents couldn't deal with the fact that I was handicapped. They weren't ready to accept that I couldn't do everything that other kids do.

I always wonder what kind of life I would have had if I hadn't been in the car accident. It's hard to think that I could have been normal.

Robbie: It would be nice to walk, but it really doesn't bother me because I've never been able to. I know people who have gotten handicapped in their teens or as adults. They're like, "This is the most horrible thing that's ever happened to me. I'm a cripple." That's what they call themselves.

My mom grew up in the hospital because back then people thought handicapped people weren't good for anything. She never really got much of an education. She would be in the hospital for a five-year period. She'd go home for a few years and then go back to the hospital. She doesn't want me to have anything like that. She wants me to be involved in as many things as I can, but I'm never really pushed to do anything I don't want to do.

Michelle: I wish I could walk. I feel bitter because I could be walking.

How do people react to disabilities?

Michelle: They just stare. They ask questions about why I'm in the chair. I like the asking. I tell them why, but they don't understand.

Elaine: Some people can't even come up to you and say, "Hi." Just because we happen to be sitting in a wheelchair doesn't mean that we're not as friendly as everybody else.

We have pretty much the same problems.

Some people come up to me and act like I am six years old. They talk to me in a, "Oh, how are you feeling today?" type attitude. Some people have come up to me and told me how courageous I was to go shopping by myself. It's really weird.

All we see are rear ends. When you're standing in line, you're right behind the person in front of you. People don't seem to think you're standing there buying anything. They cut ahead of you. I'll say, "Why don't you go behind me because I was here first? I'm waiting in line too."

Or I'll ask people to move, and they look at me and stare. Some have swore at me, and some people just won't move. I don't know what to say. I get so mad.

Debbie: A lot of times they don't see you. I have to yell, "Watch out."

Michelle: I run over some people's shoes. One time a kid was running fast down the hall. I was coming out of the room, and he landed right in my lap.

Elaine: Some people seem to disregard that we're there at all, but some overuse their kindness. At the grocery store, something might be right at my hand level, but they'll take it off the shelf for me.

Debbie: In the hall at school, they never ask you for a pass. I was in the hall, but I didn't have a pass. The woman let me go by, but I don't think it's right.

Elaine: Maybe they think we're fragile. Maybe they let it slide by because they think it might hurt us too much because we've already been through a lot.

Maple Grove, Minnesota
A private home

Grace Sandness (adoption counselor for Crossroads): When I was
hospitalized, I decided I had only one life to live, and by God, I was going to do the best I could. I tried to get control over myself and be as independent as I was able to be.

I had a friend who was willing to help me. If somebody would come and say, "Does Grace want coffee?" she'd say, "I don't know. Ask her."

You have to be assertive. The building I work in has three steps up the front. For seven years I would drive down the garage ramp. After seven years I wrote a letter to the head of the office complex. I asked, "Why don't they have a ramp at the entrance?" He said, "Why didn't you tell us sooner? We would have had one there in five minutes." That's part of the assertiveness.

I know some disabled people whom I could kick in the pants because they are riding on their disabilities. Some people sit on their buns and don't try to do anything.

My daughter is paraplegic. She follows a rock band. She's got her hair frizzed out and wears a black leather jacket and fingerless gloves. She's done a great job of eliminating her disability barriers. We have one daughter who has learning problems. She's gone through three years at the university. She studied twice as hard as anybody else.

She became an atheist because she blamed God for making her less than perfect. I believe, though, that God has a plan for my life.

Parents of handicapped kids have to band together and make sure they get what they want. All of these kids need to strive for the very best they can obtain and the very best they can do.

How do people react to handicaps?

Sandness: If kids stare at me and look at their mothers—it's trouble. The mothers will usually jerk them away. If I can get to them first with a smile or a wink, I've got it made. You have to be assertive. I've gone

so far as to race a nine-year-old boy down the supermarket aisle to prove I could run faster than he could—anything to break that gap and to put me on a common level with the other guy.

Try to ignore disabilities as much as possible. Don't be afraid of hurting somebody's feelings. We have to treat people as people.

Chicago
Metro-Chicago Easter Seals office

Hiram Zayas (director of the Gilchrist-Marchman rehabilitation center): Around 12 or 13 years old, all my peers became very body conscious. At first, I didn't understand it because from about 4 years old to 10 years old everyone is best friends. All of a sudden, you find yourself in seventh or eighth grade and things begin changing—little cliques based on physical looks.

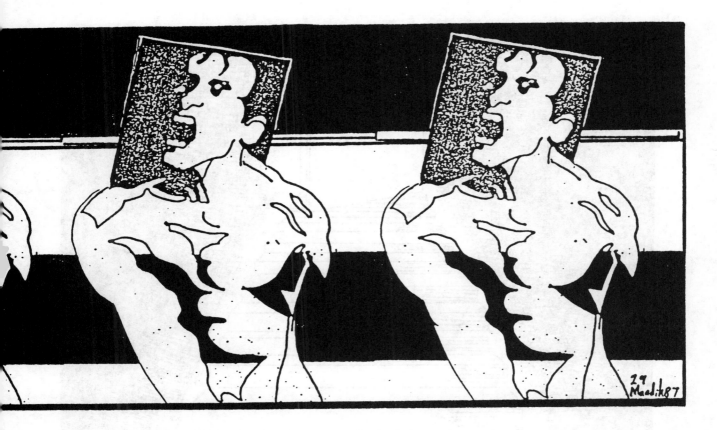

At first, it surprised me because no one really prepared me for it, talked to me about it, or informed me that this was going to happen. You experience a lot of rejection. Those years were very painful years—trying to understand about yourself: who you are, and where you fit in. So I found I had to concentrate on developing skills that other kids couldn't have. I concentrated a lot on being good academically. I was able to swim, to play bumper pool, things like that. I found out I was better in some places than the average kid. I emphasized those things to gain self-esteem.

What emotional problems must the handicapped overcome?

Zayas: Emotional pressure is common because you don't have people explaining to you what's going on. You have a tendency to withdraw. You know where you were accepted and where you

weren't so you stay away from situations that are threatening. I had little support groups of friends who remained my friends, which was nice because we kept going through adolescence together. Hardly any dating took place because the girls were so conscious of body image.

I went for my driver's license at 15 years old, and I was told that I could never drive. Somehow I met up with an older gentleman who also had no arms and a short stature. He was driving an automobile. I went over to his home to visit him to see how he fixed up his car. He took the initiative to ask me how I was doing. One of the things he shared with me was that being a teen is going to come to an end. People grow up and start thinking about other things besides the body. Adolescence is very painful unless you have somebody to talk to.

My message is, "Feel free to cry. You're only human. Accept who you are. Accept the reaction that you're having and start there. Don't try to be somebody you're not." When other handicapped people hear that, it's kind of a freeing message.

The two basic questions handicapped people have are, "Why do I go through all this suffering? Why me, God?" Catholicism teaches that you're born this way because of some sin that you did or your parents did. I grew up with that whole mentality which really screws your whole mind. When I decided to seek answers, I discovered that we are not created as a mistake. It's a uniqueness. That was liberating for me. I'm not a mistake or something that went wrong. I am beautifully and wonderfully made.

That brought me to the world view that said, "I am significant. I

can bring value to others, and there's a purpose I can serve in life. Be an example, be happy for who you are and what you can do." That sustains me. It helps me to keep going no matter how cruel people may get.

How do people react to the handicapped?

Zayas: When I went to a family picnic, I went swimming with my kids. I knew the minute I got in that pool there would be 20 to 30 kids with hundreds of questions. I dealt with it by playing with them in the pool. Playing with them helps to overcome a lot of barriers, fears, and curiosity. By the second hour, the kids didn't even bother to play with me. I answered their questions bluntly because all of their parents were on the side of the pool. The parents weren't there to go, "Shh. Shut up and don't ask." Sometimes the parents will make it more difficult because they feel uncomfortable in the situation.

What problems do the handicapped encounter?

Zayas: If it's raining, I can't hold up an umbrella so I park close to the building I'm going to. Some of the parking lots around here won't take my automobile because they can't drive it. Attitudes are changing, but it's going to take many years. I would be surprised if I feel in my lifetime no need to note differences. Two or three generations from now, possibly.

St. Louis Park, Minnesota
A private home

Barbara Berglund (affiliate, United Cerebral Palsy of Minnesota): I was born with cerebral palsy. I can't do anything with my right hand.

In college, I didn't know how to get along with people. I liked the guys, but the guys didn't like me. I had no idea what to do with a guy. The social life was frustrating. I

never learned to socialize. I had no idea what I wanted to be.

After college, I ended up back at my folks. I became isolated from my folks and from other people. It got to the point where I ended up in a home for the trainable mentally retarded whose IQ was about 50. It got so bad, it was either the home or suicide.

My professional peers don't take me seriously. When I call them up for stuff, it's generally like, "Don't bother me. You're not as important as whatever, I've got to do."

When people see me, they either shy away altogether, try to be my best friend, try to take over and run my life, or think I'm just a kid. Deep down they figure they're going to end up handicapped someday. I wish people would treat me like anybody else. But I don't think anything can be done to change people's negative attitudes because it's an individual thing.

Handicapped people cost a pretty penny. It cost my folks a lot more to raise me than if I'd been normal. We don't come cheap. We are going to live to be 70 or so like everyone else. We're not going to get unhandicapped some morning. We are going to have to be put up with or lived with. If you don't educate the handicapped, what are you going to do with them? We're not a bunch of people you can play with and then put away.

Portland, Oregon
A private home

What was your first reaction to the handicapped?

Stephanie: I was very nervous. When I was in eighth grade, we had an orientation session. They brought us a picture of the child we would be taking around. All the children had Down's syndrome. It was scary.

Jennie: I was pretty nervous

because I didn't know how to react to them and I didn't know how they were going to react to me. I didn't know what they were going to do at any time. They might do something really strange, and people would look at me like it was my fault because I'm with that person.

Stephanie: I feel bad so I overcompensate by saying, "The rest of the world has treated handicapped people so poorly so I'll try to make up for it." We aren't educated about the needs that they do have. I was with a girl who was helping a blind person who couldn't differentiate between the Pepsi and the Diet Pepsi. After she helped him, she started petting his Seeing Eye dog, which you don't do. The blind man was rather irate about it. People don't know what the handicapped's needs are.

Jennie: Most people come in contact with someone who is handicapped. The opportunity is there to learn. It doesn't have to be in classes. It may involve talking to someone who is helping that person.

Why is the public afraid of the handicapped?

Stephanie: Some handicaps are not socially accepted. People are afraid of what the handicapped might do. I've seen people lose motor control of their limbs. I've seen a mother stick her handicapped child around a pole to keep the child in place. That's frightening to me.

Jennie: People aren't as afraid of physical handicaps. If you see people in wheelchairs, it is more of a curiosity. You can anticipate what they are going to do. But if they are mentally handicapped, you don't know how mentally handicapped they are.

How do the handicapped react to able-bodied people?

Stephanie: I don't know about physically handicapped because I worked with the mentally handicapped children. They were so responsive. They were excited that the people were helping them.

Jennie: I've worked more with the physically handicapped. I'm working with one girl who just had a stroke. Her right side was paralyzed. Because she was only eight years old, she would try to take advantage of my help. She'd say, "Oh, I can't do this. Why don't you do it for me?" But as they get older, they try to do more and more.

Stephanie: After working with Special Olympics, the thing that made me so angry was abortion. They say, "The child will not live a full, healthy life." Well, the children who had Down's syndrome had the best days of their lives. How could anyone ever put a value on their lives?

Jennie: The mentally handicapped don't know any better so they are happy with what they get. The handicapped confuse society. People have all these rules, laws, and plans for able-bodied people, but when the handicapped come in and can't meet their standards, it upsets them.

Is mainstreaming helpful?

David: If the handicapped person can mainstream, that's fine. But society shouldn't have to make that many compensations for the small percent of handicapped people hanging around there.

Stephanie: I think the physically handicapped people should be mainstreamed. I've heard of programs where they have blind and deaf students in mainstreamed classes that have special adaptive measures. Obviously, the mentally handicapped are at a different level.

There is a case in California where a mother sued the school district because they wouldn't buy a $3,000 typewriter for her deaf child. The mother won.

Jennie: That's going too far.

Do the handicapped have problems socializing?

Stephanie: I haven't seen any special education kids at dances. Occasionally I see them at football games.

David: In grade school, my best friend's dad wouldn't go swimming with people he didn't know very well because he had to take off his fake leg. Once he was playing goalkeeper in a father-daughter soccer game. He punted the ball with his bad leg, and the leg flew off. That scared the hell out of some of the people. I'm sure if that happens enough, that becomes very frustrating for handicapped people.

Lombard, Illinois
Glenbard East High School

Sue: I work with a couple of handicapped guys at McDonald's. Ken, who is mentally handicapped, usually works lobby. The managers wanted him to learn something new. I was trying to teach him how to make a soft cone. When I was trying to teach him, I had to go a lot slower than if I was trying to teach a nonhandicapped person.

I've worked with Ken a long time, and I know he doesn't want to be treated like a baby. It's weird because he is really smart in sports. You could ask him who won the World Series in 1965, and he'll know. But he's slow, and his capacity for things to talk about is small. But when I go to work, I don't say real slow, "H-i, K-e-n." I just say, "Hey, Ken, what's up?" You can tell how cold he gets to people who treat him like he's different.

Then there's Steve who has a physical handicap. His arm is deformed and there are certain things that he can't do. The more friendly you are to him, the more he can make jokes about it. We have this huge garbage compactor, and

there's no way he can empty it with his arm. We joke around and say, "Steve, go empty the trash compactor." He says, "With this thing?" and holds up his arm. When I talk to him, I have to concentrate because it's hard to understand him, but it's no problem once you get used to his way of communication.

Is mainstreaming helpful?

Gerri Long (parent): Mainstreaming in a school situation can be good. Teens are much more accepting of the handicapped because in the past few years they have seen more situations with mainstreaming. When I grew up, the handicapped went to their own school. There was less interaction.

Sue: When we start talking with Ken about school, he says he "doesn't like being in class with all dumb people." He puts down other handicapped people. I don't know if it would be better for him to be in the handicapped room and excel or to be in a room with normal people and fail or not do as well.

At McDonald's, it isn't mainstreaming. The handicapped people always work in the lobby. They never work behind the counter or at the grill. Although they are yelled at or commended like anyone else, I still don't think they are mainstreamed because they are not trained to do anything else except work the lobby. Steve is discontented because he thinks that he is capable of doing more. For us, it's easy to see that he's not really capable.

What are the problems of having a handicapped friend?

Meaghan: There is this man who is in his thirties and lives behind me with his parents. When I was younger, he always liked me. I wasn't scared. I always stood there and talked with him regularly, but I couldn't have a friendship with

Marvik

handicapped go too far. The handicapped in Chicago are demanding that all CTA buses have the ramps to lift them up into a regular bus. The CTA is offering special buses that they could dial. They don't want that because that's setting them apart.

Sue: There's one retarded couple, but their baby is normal. I can't see that as being a good life to live. She probably won't realize that her parents are different until she brings them in front of her kindergarten class, and the other children make fun of them. I don't see how the parents are going to be able to deal with the girl's problems when she gets to be 17.

I can't sit here and play God and say, "You are retarded. You can't have children. You are normal. You can have children." That's not fair. But if you are retarded, why would you want to have children? I can't see going through life without feeling ashamed of your parents or feeling pain because you're different or your parents are different. They should be counseled and told that they have a chance of bringing a retarded child into this world. They should be told this is what's going to happen if your baby is retarded and this is going to happen if your baby is not retarded. You can't tell them not to have babies and not to make love because they might get pregnant, but they should be warned.

I read this article in *Reader's Digest* about this lady who knew that her child was going to be retarded. She decided to have it and said that instead of looking at it as a burden, she looked at it as a gift from God. If God thought that she couldn't handle it, He wouldn't have given it to her. She was happy to have it and willing to spend the extra time and money.

him. He still did that last summer, and my parents get a little worried that he might be hitting on me.
Sue: You feel obligated to them. For a while, Ken would say weird things to me. We have this back room where we change, and he walked back there after I had just finished changing. I said, "Oh Ken, you almost saw me change." He goes, "I'd like to see you change." My parents got a little worried, but they were more worried than I was.

I doubt that he would attack me, but I don't know if he knows saying

things like that are wrong. One time he said a really crude thing to me. I got mad and stopped talking to him for a few days. Then he asked me why I was mad. I said, "I don't like guys talking to me that way." He apologized. I taught him a lesson.

How can society help the handicapped?
Sue: We need ramps in more places. When they put the elevators in Yorktown Mall, it was a big thing. They invited all the handicapped.
Long: But sometimes the

Peggy Toews (sister of a handicapped person, special education teacher): There are times when I have to honestly deal with the fact that I would be more comfortable without certain handicapped people around, even my brother Dan. In a public situation, he may respond or do something abnormal. It has to do with pride, not wanting to be looked at or thought of differently.

I would not say that our family revolves around Danny, though that is the case in many families. A severely handicapped person is either going to pull your family together or tear it apart. It pulled us together. As I was growing up, we had babysitters a lot more than other people because Danny needed the extra care when he was younger.

Nancy Toews (mother): Danny's birth changed our way of going

30 Mardik 87

126

places for vacations. The other children were getting older so they understood more educational things, but he didn't. Therefore, we couldn't interest him. He always took more care than they did. Having a handicapped child changes a parent's life pattern.

Peggy: Most people my parents' age are free as far as responsibility for their children. But Dan is not able to be independent. Most people are free from this financial responsibility, but my dad, who is 68, and my mom, who is 64, are not and never will be free. Plus, they will die before Danny will, and they have to think about what's next for him.

How do people react to the handicapped?

Peggy: In our school, no one is openly unkind, especially not if the teacher is around. There are people who don't want to be involved so they're like, "Stay away from me." Dan knows who they are. But half the time he doesn't understand exactly what's being done to him. He doesn't open himself to being hurt.

Sometimes people feel insecure. Fears come from ignorance. I would like to put two handicapped children in every school class so the kids can spend lots of time with them. That would take care of the problem.

When I was 12 and Dan was 5 or 6, we were at church. I walked into a situation where Danny was on the ground, and two boys were picking on him. They were poking at him so I hauled off and whacked them with my purse. I felt great about it because I had my revenge, but that's not going to help the boys understand and be comfortable with the handicapped. The militant approach is not the best although it has its place.

Nancy: Danny's frustrated and angry when he's not included in something, when people try to talk

over his head, or when he doesn't understand. Danny's not capable of driving a car. It hurt for a long time because other friends his age can do that.

We worked through that and helped him accept it. "This is how God made me, and that's okay. I have certain limitations as well as everybody else." When he started at school, they put him in the ninth grade. He didn't fit in. At that age kids are not as understanding. The kids could see his needs, but they weren't willing to cooperate and understand.

Peggy: In Sunday school and church it was different. Danny felt freer. Whether they understood him or not, they accepted him. Danny helped them to accept and to understand retardation.

Nancy: I could say, "Just treat the handicapped like everyone else." Of course, that's a bad answer. People have to treat the handicapped uniquely. Just be open, and be friendly.

Olympia, Washington
Evergreen State College Summer
  Journalism Workshop

Lee (Issaquah, Washington): Some people tend to lump the handicapped into a group: "Oh they're just handicapped." But they have personalities. Some of them you might not like as much as the others, but it's just like getting to know someone else. They're more special than normal people because they have these handicaps, but they go on.

Eva (Auburn, Washington): When I meet handicapped people, I go into it thinking that they are no different than I am except that they may not be able to walk, talk as fast, or think as quickly. I talk to them normally and adjust to how they are different. They are just like ordinary people. I'm not like everyone else,

and the handicapped are not the same as I am.

Kristin (Auburn, Washington): Everyone has their handicaps. The handicapped person's handicaps are a little more evident. But I know there are things that I cannot do that other people can do, and that is a handicap.

How do people react when they meet a handicapped person?

Lee: People will tease them and give them a hard time. Sometimes the person who's handicapped doesn't even know that the person is doing it. Other people recoil: "Oh my God, what do I do? What do I say?" My boyfriend is like that. I can understand that. Some people are really uncomfortable around handicapped kids.

Eva: Sometimes it is a prejudgment. They see the handicap as an obstacle before they even talk to anyone. If someone is in a wheelchair, they don't see the person. They see the wheelchair.

How important are handicapped parking spaces?

Stacy: My dad is in a wheelchair, and he has to park in those.

Lee: It makes me mad to see cars without the disabled sticker parking there. It's like you just want to go up to them and key their car.

Laura: It's no skin off our backs to give them a few parking spaces. It's so much easier for them and helps them fit into society.

How can society break down the stereotypes?

Lee: People can find handicapped people and interview them, like "20/20" or the Barbara Walters specials, and have America look. It would break down a lot of barriers.

Eva: I think that the media tend to cover only the bad side. There was a school with kids who had special problems; they were really extreme cases. The state was trying to teach the kids. When the media concentrate on the handicapped, they pick out all the bad things.

Lee: A thing that bugs me is the babies born with massive congenital defects—spina bifida, babies that need shunts to drain their brains. I can understand letting some die a natural death like God intended. But there are some cases when if you can do anything to give that child a chance at a normal life, go for it.

Sometimes it makes me mad that doctors try so hard to save this baby when all that it is going to be doing is lying in bed. It doesn't seem like much of a life. I don't see why doctors should make that choice of who is going to live and who is going to die.

One of the things that you have to think about when you know your child is going to be born with congenital defects is how it is going to affect your marriage and your other kids. It can break up marriages. It might be playing God, but at some time you have to put yourself first. And if it is best for you and your family to let that baby die, then I totally understand that.

Compiled by Kim Peirce

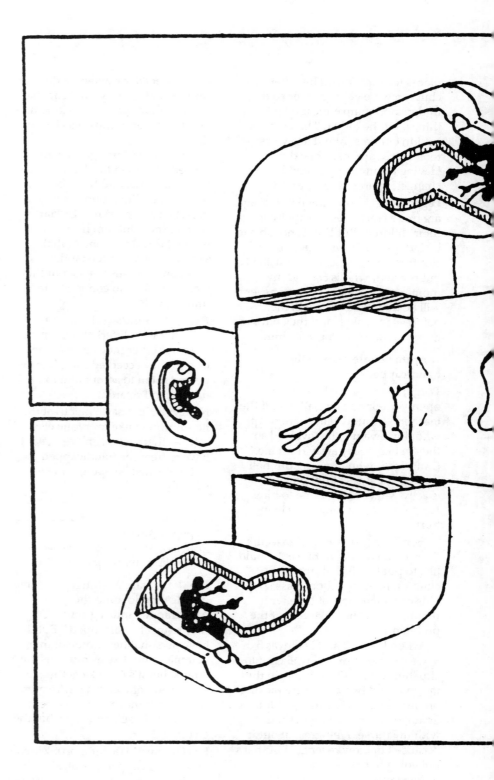

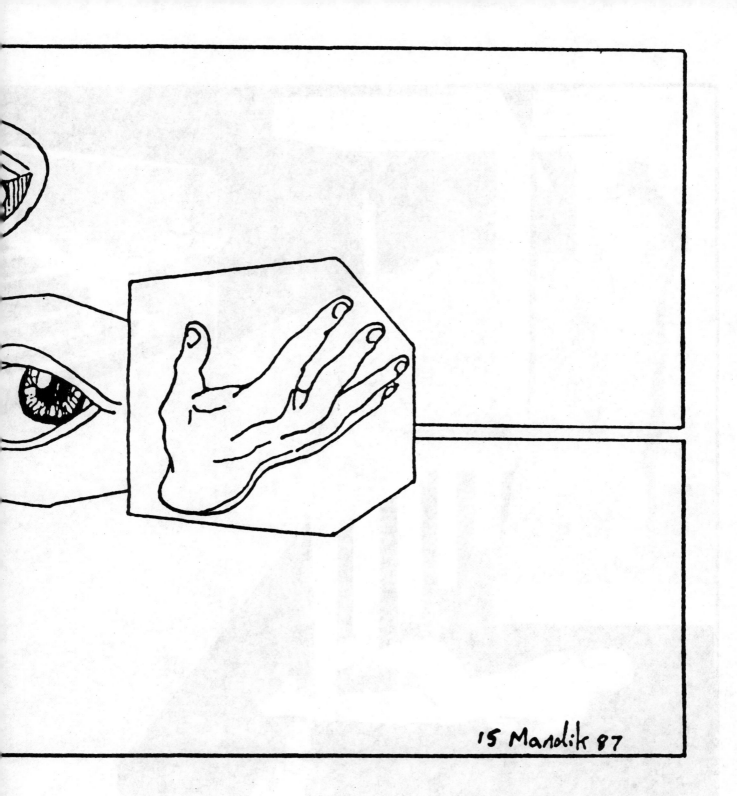

15 Mandlik 87

Nonhandicapped and Handicapped   *129*

Solutions

Before we can say what the right reaction is to a handicapped person, we should try to figure out what good this person is to our society and economic standing in the United States. A handicapped person costs the taxpayers money which they have worked hard for. Most handicapped people cannot benefit our working class or our economy in any way.

Is there a right way to react to handicapped people? How does it make you feel when the government is putting your tax dollars back into the special help organizations? . . . . The "right way" to react is not to react at all. Let them be and make it on their own. The only difference should be in the way they look, not the way they are treated.

No one else gets special treatment so why should they? In America's free enterprise system, one should be able to keep the money he or she earns.

> Cris Cruz, 17
> Hillsdale, Michigan

I have a brother who's handicapped, and I didn't even see a difference between him and the rest of the world until I was close to 11. In fact, I found out because a bully on the block said my brother was retarded. I laughed in his face, but later I asked my mom about it. She said he wasn't retarded, but he has cerebral palsy and epilepsy.

I actually had gone through 11 years knowing what to do during seizures but never realizing he was any different from anyone else.

He leads an active life and has two kids and a wife. How is he different? Yes, he takes medicine, has to have special medical coverage, and has a limp, but so do a lot of other people. . . . I respect him because he respects himself.

> Laura Hatcher, 17
> Idaho Falls, Idaho

When I see those people in wheelchairs, I feel like I'm going to burst out in tears. Even though I complain about the parking spaces, I realize that they are reserved for the handicapped because they need it.

I knew a little girl, age six, and she told me, "It ain't that easy being handicapped. Everyone looks at you." Just think how sad it would be if the public ignored them.

Susan Cha, 17
San Francisco, California

There is a state home not far from here that I visited with a class. Some of us were not prepared enough for what we might see. When one of the patients would approach, . . . my classmate would shrink back as if in fear. This hurt the patient's feelings. It's like you're saying to him, "Get away from me, you freak. Don't you dare lay a hand on me." These people are not out to hurt anyone. They just want the love and compassion they deserve.

I have an uncle who has Down's syndrome. He is the most loving and caring person I've ever known. He is very cheerful and hardly anything gets him down .

At first I was embarrassed to be around him, and I'm ashamed to admit it. Before, I would do anything not to be around him. I thought of him as someone who would hurt me. But somehow the messages of love broke through the hostility held within my heart. I opened my eyes up to see a very loving and caring person. . . .

The handicapped. . .want to give love, but no one will let them. What this world needs is love, and it's just around the corner dwelling in the handicapped's heart. All we have to do to help them express their love is hold our hand out and let them know that despite their handicap, they're loved just the same. Try it sometime. It will give you a warmth of satisfaction that makes you feel good that you've allowed yourself to be loved and you loved back.

Robin Porter, 17
Hillsdale, Michigan

Many problems can be caused by the special privileges that are given to handicapped individuals. When you walk in a restroom, there is always a special stall for handicapped people. It's kind of a pain when all the other stalls are filled and you have to use that stall. The same problem is presented with parking spaces. It's a pain when you are in a hurry and the only parking space left is reserved for the handicapped.

This was never a problem for our family because we had a handicapped aunt living with us. So we had a sign for our car that gave us legal permission to use the handicapped parking spaces. We still have this sign even though my aunt died and still use it when we have to sometimes.

I think we could resolve some of these problems by making separate restrooms for handicapped individuals. . . . I don't think parking spaces should be segregated. It is just as much a pain for us to walk a little ways to a store as it is for them to wheel themselves there.

I do feel sorry for them, but we all have handicaps of our own and we aren't given special privileges for them so why should they? We have to bear with them and learn to live with them so I think they should too. Maybe we could resolve some problems by just giving these special privileges to the very handicapped, not to those who are only slightly handicapped.

> 15-year-old female
> Iowa

Handicapped people are not inferior. If anything, they are superior. They try to help you. They go out of their way to cheer you up.

Recently I had the chance to become involved with handicapped children. They made me feel so special, like I was important. They taught me to appreciate things I took for granted—like a flower. I was passing out flowers to people who were entering a benefit for the handicapped, and a girl came up to receive her flower. I gave it to her, and her eyes filled with tears. She said, "Thank you, I love it."

Later, inside at the dance, the king and queen of the Peppermint Twist were being announced. The handicapped children had won—four girls in the court, one king, and one queen. The king and queen danced to their victory song. Tears filled my eyes as the singer sang, "Glory, Glory, Alleluia." It was a touching moment I'll never forget. They walked down the stage and were both crying because they were so happy.

I wish our community could have projects like this so that others could make the breakthrough I have. Just because they're handicapped doesn't make them inhuman.

> Lynn Racine, 17
> Willow Springs, Illinois

When we were young, we were all told not to stare. Don't look at those people in wheelchairs or those missing limbs.

When we became older, the word handicap was introduced to our vocabulary. Handicap is a word with the same effect on us as disease. You stare away, ignoring the "special people."

People with disabilities are not special. They are people, people capable of love and almost anything else a "normal" person can do.

Turning away doesn't help the situation. It only shows how people are not caring. The only people who aren't turning away are the young children who are naive to society's prejudice.

A better name for handicapped would be physically challenged. The close-minded ignoring crowd are the ones who should be labeled as handicapped.

Special treatment is not necessary. Challenged people can cope. If they are in need of help, they will ask.

> Gary Hood, 17
> Idaho Falls, Idaho

Afterword

When teens examine the world of peers, they discover the divergence between what they see and what they perceive. Never verbalized but implicitly understood, their realization that the appearance and the reality differ causes the stress and the strain that molds the lives of modern teenagers.

Teenagers naturally experience confusion. The world that they see—the adult world—bears no resemblance to the world that they know—the real world. They believe that most adults sidestep the reality and prefer to accept the appearance: the status quo. But teens demand interpretation, not simple observation. Explanation, not fabrication. Correction, not toleration.

Even though they are inexperienced, teens sense that the solutions lie in communication—honestly expressing the hurts, the confusion, the crises, and the triumphs. Teenagers also realize that they must take up the gauntlet and charge beyond the talk, to bring minority friends to racist neighborhoods, to challenge apparently insurmountable language barriers, to overcome physical challenges, to survive when friends die in gang warfare, to seek answers where answers seemingly cannot be found.

Yes, teenagers are concerned about the issues. Yes, teenagers seem apathetic, but only because they lack direction. Yes, teenagers want to communicate, to open the doors to the solutions that could be. Yes, teenagers realize that the choice is theirs—to heed the voices of conflict and to fulfill the promise of dreams. Yes, teenagers know that they have just begun the process.

Greg Jao

National Teenage Research Project staff:
Doug Addison, Chris Anderson, Sara Corrough, Doug Elwell,
Robert Hester, Greg Jao, Michelle Jao, Erik Landahl, Pete Mandik,
Cathy Mau, Gina Nolan, Mark Peaslee, Kim Peirce, Paulette
Polinski, Dave Seng, Diana Slyfield, assistant coordinator; Howard
Spanogle, director.

Copy consultant:
Christine Zrinsky

Research aides:
Kristin Jass and Juanita Spanogle

Summer volunteers:
Neville Bilimoria, Vicki Dominick, Pat Bowlin, Susan Drechsel, Debbie
Elifson, Meaghan Emery, Julio Flores, Jackie Freer, Ruth Grunewald,
Peggy Iffland, Rob Kengott, Bill Karrow, David Markines, Julie Murphy,
Dave Palomares, Lisa Seidlitz, Janice Shoulders, Forrest Slyfield, Jennifer
Sullivan, Jennifer Sweda, Kristin Walz, Jeannie Wang, Sam Woo

Additional Echo staff, 1985-87; Journalism students, 1986-87:
John Alexis, Amy Baker, Mike Balgemann, Amy Bartt, Viren Bavishi, Shirish
Bhatt, Smita Bhatt, Jeannine Brechin, Tim Burke, Steve Fisher, Jeffrey Freeman,
Karen Glyzewski, Don Gomez, Chris Gorman, Ada Gutierrez, Christie Hart,
Brad Herbert, Carolyn Holland, Jon Johnson, Tasia Katinas, Rebecca
Kniebusch, Christine Kosman, Karen Long, Mark Ludena, Walt Martinez, Chris
Morache, Ginger Murphy, Kathleen O'Connor, Corey Poris, Charlie Reiman, Sean
Sampey, Gerald Shepardson, Debby Stowell, Tammy Thorp, Jon Tyndall, JoAnn
Vasbinder, Gary Wang, Patty Weyburn